Instructor's Manual
for
Tools for Writing

Using the Natural Human Learning Process

Rita Smilkstein, Ph.D.

North Seattle Community College

Printed in the United States of America

ISBN: 0–15–503094–9

7 8 9 0 1 2 3 4 5 6 054 9 8 7 6 5 4 3 2 1

Table of Contents

INTRODUCTION

The goal of this course is to enable students to express their ideas in grammatically correct standard English—and to know exactly what they are doing and how to do it. Subgoals include making students proficient in number agreement and in identifying and correcting sentence boundary errors. Students will also have the metacognitive awareness needed for being proficient self-evaluators.

Because this curriculum is planned for one course, there is hardly time to cover the elements and structures even minimally needed to write correct standard English sentences. The curriculum, therefore, is guided by the following principles:

1. Rushing through the whole world of writing and trying to cover everything students need to learn is counterproductive.
2. Until and unless a firm foundation of basic standard English sentence grammar is constructed, little further progress can be made.
3. Constructing this firm foundation is the first and most essential step for these students.
4. All elements not essential for constructing this foundation must be left out.

This is an entirely new approach to teaching developmental students how to write grammatically correct sentences. It is based on how the brain naturally learns (the **Natural Human Learning Process**) and on students' natural ability to succeed when they have the opportunity to learn and think in a way that is compatible with the **Natural Human Learning Process**. Students who regularly attend class and regularly do their homework show dramatic improvement. Moreover, students enjoy this curriculum and approach, a conclusion attested to by the extraordinarily high retention rate—between 90 percent and 100 percent.

The Students

There are three types of students who will benefit from this student-centered, student-active, **Natural Human Learning Process** grammar curriculum.

1. *Native-speaking basic (developmental or remedial) writers.* Typically, these are students for whom the written sentence is an undifferentiated jumble and grammar rules a mystery. However, they also have a profound desire to acquire skill with the written language, something they have so far failed to do and perhaps have despaired of ever learning to do. Some basic writing students think they are stupid. But students' success with this difficult, challenging curriculum shows just how intelligent and motivated they really are.

Some of these students have grown up speaking nonstandard English or a nonstandard dialect of English. Consequently, they cannot depend on their ear to know what standard English sounds like. But they can depend on their sense of logic and their analytical and synthesizing thinking abilities. This curriculum depends on students having these mental abilities, which the teacher can assume are innate in every human being whose brain is not severely impaired.

2. *ESL students in basic writing courses.* These students often have good rote or theoretical grammar knowledge and can do well in workbook exercises and on standardized grammar tests; some are even highly literate in their native language. However, their writing in English does not reflect this knowledge. These ESL students cannot identify in their own writing the same structures and elements they can expertly identify in a workbook exercise, nor can they correct in their own writing the errors they can easily correct in the workbook exercises.

These students, like the first group (and deaf students, of course), cannot depend on their ear to know what standard English is and, thus, need the kind of intensive, sustained, active, and interactive practice and processing provided in this curriculum.

3. *Freshman composition students.* Often students placed in regular composition classes need some grammar work to support their proofreading and editing. These students can run through this curriculum very quickly (in approximately five to ten sessions) because they already have internalized grammar understanding. In the course for which this curriculum has been designed, however, students might need the entire term to reach proficiency with the concepts and skills in just the first eight chapters.

The Curriculum—and the Course for Which It Was Designed

The course for which this curriculum has been primarily designed is the introductory, sentence-level, basic English course for the first two types of students described in the preceding section. Students should be assigned to this course on the basis of a writing sample that shows they lack understanding of the rules of grammatically correct standard English. Their scores on a reading test might indicate a sixth grade or lower reading level.

In this curriculum, students do not read books or articles; they do not read and discuss their writing—either their own or their classmates'—for any purpose other than to explore whether their sentences are grammatically correct. However, even though this curriculum focuses exclusively on sentence-level grammar and does not address rhetorical, writing-process, or compositional concerns, students are regularly writing short pieces in class and for homework. In this way they continually practice expressing their ideas and feelings in writing.

Amazingly, as their understanding and confidence increase, so does their ability to write logically and clearly about complex ideas—even without instruction in how to do this. Vocabulary and spelling also improve without instruction. Moreover, some students say that, when they learn how to write with dependent clauses and relative clauses (Chapters 7 and 8), they can express their feelings and ideas in words for the first time in their life.

Finally, this curriculum does not teach grammar rules. Instead it gives students grammar tools for writing sentences. As students gain skill at using their *tools*, they become better able to write correct sentences. Tools are empowering. This curriculum aims to put tools into the hands of students.

Furthermore, these tools are presented in functional, commonsensical terminology so they will make immediate and logical sense to the student. As suggested in the following sections, tools can be introduced by writing them on the chalkboard or using an overhead projector; transparency masters for the tools are in the back of this manual. Students then copy the tools into their book, in effect helping to write their own textbook. Students rate this approach to the textbook most highly.

However, because common sense and functional terminology is used in most cases rather than the conventional terminology, students need to know the conventional terms so they can communicate with subsequent teachers. For this reason, a glossary that includes equivalent terminology is provided at the end of the textbook.

Organization of the Chapters

OVERVIEW

Chapter 1 focuses on the development of students' metacognitive knowledge of how they learn and how to facilitate and be responsible for their own learning. Self-evaluation tools begin each chapter after Chapter 1.

The second chapter begins the grammar work with prepositional phrases. This is done for two reasons:

1. Prepositional phrases are the simplest self-contained structures or units of thought in a sentence; thus, they are an accessible—rather than a daunting—introduction to grammar. Students immediately begin to feel grammar-empowered and confident as they begin working on prepositional phrases by this **Natural Human Learning Process** approach, which focuses on logic and commonsense rather than on theory.

2. When students can recognize the prepositional phrases in their sentences, it is easier for them to identify the subjects and verbs.

Chapters 3, 4, and 5 focus on subjects and verbs, subject-verb word order, auxiliary and main verbs, verbals, and number agreement. Tense is introduced. Chapter 6 introduces pronouns and a uniting concept—subject-verb completers—for direct and indirect objects and complements. Why call all these different elements "subject-verb completers"? Because distinguishing among these different elements does not empower students to write correct sentences. What does help them write correctly is their ability to recognize the subject and verb and the words that complete their meaning. The concept of subject-verb completer does this logically, relying on students' ability to think commonsensically.

The culminating seventh and eighth chapters comprise concepts and tools for handling clauses (dependent, independent, and relative) and sentence boundaries. By Chapter 7, students will have acquired the foundational concepts and skills needed for the more sophisticated and complex work in these two chapters.

The next four chapters (9 through 12) focus in more detail on tenses, pronouns, and punctuation. These chapters also include sections on adverbs and adjectives. Chapter 12 addresses some of the common problems of ESL students: articles, verbals, and idioms.

RATIONALE

This book leaves the more detailed and in-depth account of tenses, pronouns, and punctuation to the last four chapters. Because there is not enough time in a single, sentence-level grammar course for students to firmly acquire concepts and skills concerning every element in the sentence, the basic foundational concepts predominate. Thus the book is organized so that students are assured of firmly acquiring at least the most basic concepts (Chapters 2 through 8). Therefore, the minimum goal is to reach the end of Chapter 8 by the end of the term.

Chapters 9 through 11 are included for students who are prepared or advanced enough to proceed more quickly through the earlier chapters. Alternatively, selected parts of these chapters can be used as needed for extra in-class work or as assignments for individual students with specific problems. Chapter 12 might be assigned to ESL students for individual or small-group work, also on an as-needed basis.

Because of the time problem, spelling and vocabulary are not included in this course. Some ESL and development programs link a basic writing course with a basic reading course in an integrated program, which, of course, makes it possible to include more than can be learned in any single, stand-alone course.

Questions and Answers

Here are some of the questions I have been asked about this approach and the answers I have given.

QUESTION: Why "tools" and not "rules"?

ANSWER: Basic writing students tend to have a negative attitude about grammar rules. Also, one connotation of rules is that they constrict and limit behavior. On the other hand, tools are useful and helpful for making and producing things. The word *tools* connotes activity, craft, skill, creativity. This is a new and refreshing way to think about learning grammar—using it, getting a handle on it, controlling it, making it into something the user wants.

QUESTION: In this curriculum, teachers introduce the tools by writing them on the chalkboard or showing them on an overhead projector and then having the students copy them into their book. Why have students copy down the tools when they are printed in the book?

ANSWER: When students copy down the tools written by the teacher on the board, they are immediately making a personal, physical connection. When they later see these tools in their own handwriting in their own book that they are writing, they experience a feeling of ownership. Also, the tools that the teacher will write on the board as given in the Instructor's Manual are often worded slightly differently from those in the printed version. This gives students the idea that the *meaning* rather than the rote memorization of the tools is important.

QUESTION: Isn't it too confusing and difficult for students to do so much detailed analyzing with so many abbreviations? Doesn't it drive them crazy or bore them?

ANSWER: No. Students learn the coding bit by bit and practice a great deal before they go on. The analyses are scaffolds that help strengthen students' understanding and control over the elements and structures of their sentences. Teachers are always surprised at how pleased students are at being able to do this work. They enjoy the stimulation and challenge. They feel their power and control growing. It is something specific they can do to get a handle on what is otherwise an undifferentiated mass of uncontrollable words. And as students get control of each element or structure, they can stop analyzing that element or structure, and the scaffolding can begin to disappear.

QUESTION: Isn't this too different and complicated for me to just start teaching it without intensive training?

ANSWER: You will no doubt feel more confident and comfortable if you do get some training first. However, teachers who have not been trained have taught this and have done well and enjoyed it, especially when they have seen how quickly and positively their students have responded. They have told me that it takes at least one time through to see how the program works. A number of teachers who weren't trained have written and phoned with questions. I have included in the Comments sections that end the lesson plans for each chapter in this manual all their questions and concerns. I hope these comments will serve as troubleshooting guides.

QUESTION: Why allow students to call infinitives prepositional phrases in Chapter 2? Why make up terms like *subject-verb completers* for complements and direct and indirect objects? Why not specify that prepositional phrases are modifiers? And why not include with the subject all its modifiers, including prepositional phrases?

ANSWER: The purpose of this course is to help students get a handle on sentence elements and structures. Its method is to build foundations and then construct concepts and skills upon those basic foundations. Its approach is to have students rely on their logic and common sense and be able to understand everything clearly and to see patterns, elements, and structures in sentences.

Therefore, until students know about verbs and verbals they will not grasp what infinitives are. Distinctions between predicate nouns, predicate adjectives, direct and indirect objects, and the various uses of prepositional phrases take more time to make—and are of more interest theoretically than practically—than the benefits they yield for gaining control over the sentence. And being able to see *whole* structures and elements, like the subject and all its modifiers as one structure, helps students see what is going on in a sentence—and control the sentence—more than just being able to identify isolated words.

QUESTION: Won't students lose their motivation if the focus is only on their grammar and not their ideas?

ANSWER: No. For these students, gaining power and control over their sentences, knowing what they're doing and how to do it, is heady, exhilarating, satisfying. They do get feedback on their writing when I write comments on their homework and in-class essays. These comments, though, are not for the purpose of evaluating or improving their writing. They are solely for the purpose of supporting the students in their efforts to gain grammar power. Students are highly motivated to learn all the grammar they can in this class so they can do well in their upcoming writing classes.

QUESTION: Are these students motivated to learn this grammar? Do they see it as relevant?

ANSWER: Yes! Better than anyone, they know the value and necessity of having grammar power and control over their sentences. Unfortunately, learning grammar has usually been theoretical, abstract, workbook-centered, rule-based. This approach, to the contrary, engages students' interest, gives them hope, and makes it possible for them to learn and succeed.

QUESTION: If students write their own textbook, isn't it possible that there will be mistakes?

ANSWER: All mistakes are quickly seen and corrected because of the ongoing assessment of the homework and in-class work. Students write homework for each class. During class, students are working and showing what they know and don't know. Corrections are continually being made. This flexible approach allows students to grow and learn in a natural, individually oriented way.

QUESTION: Is it a good idea to teach students about negatives like sentence boundary errors or error recognition? Isn't it better to present only correct models?

ANSWER: Because students do make mistakes and learn to write correctly by correcting their mistakes, it is important for them to recognize their own mistakes. Because they commit sentence boundary errors, they need to be able to see them and know how to correct them. Even we, who know how to write correctly, sometimes make mistakes. Don't we all need to proofread, to scan our writing to find our errors so we can correct them?

QUESTION: Why is there no instruction on essay writing?

ANSWER: There isn't any time. Is it better to cover many things superficially or focus on constructing a strong, clear foundation of knowledge and skill? This book takes the position that, with the former approach, students will always suffer from gaps in their knowledge and will limp along through their writing courses. With the latter approach, however, students will have a solid, firm foundation upon which they can later construct their writing skill and knowledge. Students, though, do a great deal of writing in this curriculum, both in class and as homework. Moreover, near the end of each chapter is an in-class essay writing assignment.

QUESTION: Why isn't there more attention paid to the needs of ESL students?

ANSWER: This course is intended for ESL students who have gone through the basic ESL courses. By the time they enter this course, they should be more or less at a par with native speakers. There are several sentence elements, however, that are continuing problems for ESL students; these elements (verbals, articles, and idioms) are presented in a special chapter for ESL students, Chapter 12.

Introduction to the Natural Human Learning Process: Metacognitive Activity and Lecture

Being aware of how they learn and how well they are doing helps students gain control over and take responsibility for their own learning. Thus, many self-evaluation and self-awareness activities are provided. Specifically, each chapter after Chapter 1 begins with a Review Problem and a Knowledge Evaluation. The Review Problem can be used as a quiz or as a study question with students referring to the previous chapter for the answer. The Knowledge Evaluation section comprises both a self-evaluation for the knowledge gained in the previous chapter as well as a self-evaluation for the knowledge to be gained in the new chapter. These self-evaluations give students the opportunity to reflect on and contrast their level of knowledge before and after each chapter. There is also an optional evaluation tool on page 37 that can be used on an overhead projector or duplicated and handed out to each student.

Chapter 1 contains a metacognitive activity that introduces students to how they learn. Supplementary material gives step-by-step directions for conducting this activity, which can be given on the first or second day of the course. This self-awareness activity never fails to encourage and raise the self-confidence of students, especially developmental students. This metacognitive knowledge about how their mind learns helps them immensely, not only affectively but also cognitively; now they know the steps they must go through (or put themselves through if the teacher does not) to learn anything new and to improve in something they are beginning to learn.

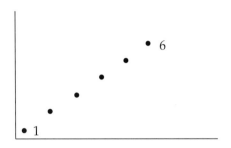

This shorthand diagram on the chalkboard introduces students to a self-evaluation (and teacher evaluation) method relating to the **Natural Human Learning Process** diagram introduced earlier.

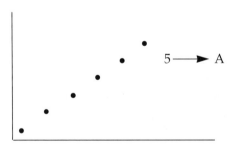

This **NHLP** diagram might also be used by the teacher to evaluate student work, such as the in-class essays. This diagram can be drawn on each student's essay and the grade related to the **Natural Human Learning Process**: 5, 6 = A; 4 = B; 3 = C; 2 = D; 1 = F.

The Underlying Theory and Research

This curriculum or approach is based on a belief in students' ability to learn and their desire to learn. Both theory and research tell us that human beings are born to learn, are impelled by their brain to learn.

Schema Theory

A schema is a mental picture or concept or understanding of something we know well or something we can do with skillfulness. For example, how do you know when you are in a classroom? You have a concept of what a classroom looks like that is composed of the elements you have experienced in, and associate with, classrooms. Similarly, you also have schemas for other kinds of rooms, like kitchens, concert halls, restaurants, dentists' offices.

Let us say someone blindfolds you, leads you into a room, then removes the blindfold and asks you where you are. You will begin to match the elements you see around you to the various room schemas in your mind: There's a low stage in front with rows of seats in a semicircle facing the stage, but there is no chalkboard. Maybe it's a small concert hall. Then you see a movable chalkboard in the corner: It's probably a classroom.

And when you write a sentence, how do you know it is not a fragment or a run-on? If you have rich schemas for sentence boundaries in your mind, you match (consciously or unconsciously) the elements in your particular, never-written-before sentence with the elements of sentence-boundary schemas in your mind. If you find a match, you know there is no sentence boundary error. If it does not match, you know what matching element(s) the sentence needs.

Writers need many complex and interrelating schemas in their minds if they are to know whether their sentences are grammatically correct and, when not, how to make them correct. If writers do not have these schemas in their mind, how can they know whether their sentences are correct? By this theory, they cannot. According to schema theory, it is not possible for people to understand unless they have the relevant schema(s) in their mind. Moreover, each separate schema is exquisitely experience- or learning-specific, and writers need one or more schemas for each and every grammar concept or skill.

Thus, the task before the grammar teacher is how to get grammar schemas into a student's mind. Teachers usually try to do this by having students memorize grammar rules, practice applying these rules in workbooks, and then, magically, transfer the rules to their own writing. But, as we know, this does not work for many developmental students.

One feature of the rule-memorizing, workbook-based approach that might seem indispensable to instructors faced with a classful of students making a daunting amount of egregious grammar errors is that the entire class needs to work on the same exercises.

Otherwise, how can teachers teach the same thing to the whole class? This **NHLP** curriculum and approach, however, solves this problem by making it possible for all students to construct the same new schemas even as each one authentically expresses his or her own ideas in his or her own never-written-before sentences.

Constructivism and Brain Physiology

Constructivist theory and brain physiology help us understand how people construct their schemas. Constructivist theory, based on Piaget's work, posits that only by direct, active, personal experiences (trial and error, groping and correcting) can a person construct new schemas—that is, learn. Neuroplastic research (research about changes that occur in the brain during learning) tells us that there is a physiological basis for this theory: Brain nerve cell structures grow and connect during constructivist activities. Specifically, as a person practices, brain nerve cell fibers, called *dendrites*, grow; and new connections, called *synapses*, are formed between brain nerve cells. This is the physiological phenomenon that underlies learning. The following paragraphs might be considered a gloss, albeit still oversimplified, on Chapter 1 (see the figures in Chapter 1).

At the beginning of learning something new, the learner is devoid of a schema; that is, the learner's brain is devoid of the dendrites and synapses for that specific object of learning (concept or skill). This lack is concomitant with the learner's having no capacity for understanding or even seeing this object of learning, much less for using or applying it, except insofar as it resembles schemas that have already been constructed about something else, except insofar as there already exists a neural network of dendrites and synapses from previous practice and experience with a similar skill or concept.

In fact, previously acquired neural networks will be the key to acquiring new ones, since new dendrites must attach to and grow from existing dendrites. Physical structures do not grow out of nothing; they grow off existing structures. According to Piaget, our very first learning attaches to or grows from our innate reflexes; from these first connections, all else, all other learning, grows (also see Fischbach, 1992).

As previously discussed, a learner constructs a neural network by actively practicing (working with, thinking about, analyzing, reflecting on) his or her own personal, direct experiences, starting with simple activities and progressing through several levels of increasingly complex activities:

1. Students need to be made ready to learn by stimulating and, thus, preparing their existing dendrites for new growth. This is done by giving students a task that they can accomplish with their existing understanding and that will be a basis on which to construct the new understanding.

2. Learners need personal, authentic experiences at a beginning level that allow them to actively practice tasks experimentally, groping and correcting by trial and error. In this way, dendrites for the new skill

or concept will begin to be constructed as students get acquainted with the superficial aspects of the new object of learning.

3. Learners now need more personal, authentic practice to become more familiar and comfortable with the superficial aspects of the new object of learning. Further active practice increases students' dendrite growth, concomitant with an increase in their understanding and skill. The neural network is now rich enough to be a basis for more complex, in-depth, finer-tuned understanding and skill. Throughout this learning process, dendrites and synapses are forming into more and more complex neural networks, concomitant with more complex understanding (Petit & Markus, 1987).

4. Now learners need and are able to do more complex, sophisticated tasks. These tasks make it possible for students to fine-tune and enrich their neural network further, concomitant with understanding the object of learning in greater detail and depth and being able to use the new understanding with increasing fluency and skill. (In other courses lectures and reading assignments, if relevant, will now be understood and appreciated. Before this stage, lectures and reading assignments usually will deliver only rote or verbal knowledge. However, in this curriculum there are no reading assignments and no formal lectures.)

5. Learners are now ready for even higher-level tasks. Their neural network has developed from an initial lack of brain structure growth, concomitant with superficial understanding about an object of learning, to proliferated dendrite growth, concomitant with sophisticated, in-depth, understanding (Jacobs, Schall, & Scheibel, 1993).

6. Continuing practice will create an even richer, more refined schema and neural network, concomitant with even more fluent skill and creative understanding. Students can continue to improve this understanding and skill over time. It is now a neural network from which new, more complex ones can be constructed and which can be synthesized with other, already-formed networks.

Neuroplastic research shows that brain structures are constructed or "tailor-made" with exquisite precision for what a learner is actively practicing and processing. Research also tells us that schemas and neural networks are not transferable; they work only for the skill or concept for which they were precisely and specifically constructed. For example, as we know, students do not transfer their workbook grammar knowledge to their own writing. This is because students who are learning grammar through workbooks are constructing workbook neural networks. In order to construct their own-writing neural networks, they must learn grammar through their own writing.

Synthesis (neural meta-networking), on the other hand, occurs between two or more networks that have already been constructed or are being constructed. Synthesis of several well-developed networks allows people to see relationships between tasks, ideas, or situations and to use understanding from one situation in a different situation.

The Process

The practice and processing learners do must be very active—the more active, the more neural growth, the more schema construction, the more learning. A challenge to the constructivist, **NHLP** teaches us how to increase student activity in the classroom.

In order to turn the activity and processing level up as high as possible to facilitate neural growth, this curriculum uses a three-step sequence of heightened activity and interactivity:

1. Each learning experience begins with students completing a task individually. Each student thus consults his or her own unique mind and stimulates his or her own idiosyncratic neural networks and schemas: Because each has a different history, each will have his or her own different mindstore of schemas and neural networks. This step might take one to five minutes or more, depending on the task. The teacher can have students move to the next step when at least half are finished.

2. Students next meet in small groups of three or four for five to ten minutes. They share and discuss their written work. They might ask for assistance from the instructor, who, otherwise, can help them most by keeping out of their way. The small groups give students the opportunity to interactively process. They talk and listen, hear other perspectives, reflect, analyze, compare, contrast, and give and receive peer tutoring. Some of the most important learning in the class takes place in these small groups.

Research has shown that peer tutoring is one of the most effective ways to learn. It is important to share with students the fact that, when students work in groups and tutor and help each other, those who tutor seem to gain more than those being tutored.

Students might stay in the same group throughout the course, or they might benefit from being in groups with different people. The teacher can best judge what will be most helpful for the students.

Members of groups finishing early might be asked to put their work on the chalkboard for group critique and discussion in the next step, a whole-group debriefing. The teacher can have students move to the next activity when about half the groups are finished.

3. Students then reassemble as a whole group. If none of the small groups finished early enough to write their work on the board, individual volunteers might now be asked to do so. The tools involved should continuously be reviewed and discussed to further facilitate students' network construction. Students are emboldened to take risks when the teacher makes it clear that people learn by making and correcting mistakes and that a student who makes a sincere mistake on the board is doing the class a service because everyone can learn from that mistake. Questions are asked and answered. New information or tools might be given.

This whole-group debriefing and instructional session maintains a high level of activity for continuous learning, strengthens community interactivity, and gives the instructor a picture of the overall level of understanding of the specific concept being taught.

As students proceed through the curriculum, their understanding develops cumulatively, with new, more complex networks connected to and constructed on the previous ones. Their grammar dendrites grow fuller and richer, activity by activity. As a result, their writing is slowly improving—and they know exactly what they are doing and how to do it.

However, it is critical not to underestimate the amount of time and effort it takes for students to become skillful at recognizing and correctly using sentence elements and structures. It is essential that students have sufficient opportunities and time to do the practice needed to construct a firm foundation, which is the prerequisite for successful learning and further progress. These students are constructing new brain structures; this is difficult work, especially for these students, many of whom are suffering from repeated past failures and lack of confidence.

What This Approach Is and What It Isn't

Because this **NHLP** approach might be confused with or incorrectly compared to some other approaches, it is necessary to discuss how it differs.

This is not a behaviorist or Skinner-type approach, nor even a Bloomian mastery learning approach. One difference is that behaviorist and mastery learning approaches both are essentially workbook approaches whereas this **Natural Human Learning Process** approach helps students construct schemas as they work on their own authentic writing. Another difference is that, in this **NHLP** approach, each element and structure is seen as complex, and the whole complex element or structure (for example, the prepositional phrase) is taught both analytically and holistically.

The **NHLP** approach does include an analytical aspect even though the analytical learn-one-small-element-at-a-time approach is criticized by those who say that children learn to speak, read, and write holistically. Therefore, teaching writing to adults should also be holistic. Unfortunately, research shows that the holistic approach alone does not work with adult developmental students (Hillocks, 1986; Kroll & Vann, 1981).

Adult basic writing students are often limited to only one or a few basic writing courses in which to acquire the foundation neural networks that skillful writers have had many years to develop. In the twelve years from kindergarten through high schools, some students successfully learned the grammar elements and structures and "naturally" became able to write correctly. But our adult basic writing students do not have the time for natural, holistic acquisition of grammar schemas in the same way.

Furthermore, reading- and writing-centered approaches are suitable for a different type of student, a student who already has basic writing grammar understanding but whose writing is stilted, awkward, wordy, inauthentic, grandiose, or unclear.

Our student, on the other hand, is one who does not have basic writing grammar understanding. Basic writing grammar is profoundly complex and does not evolve on its own. Basic writing students first need to construct foundation grammar networks. Then reading- and writing-centered approaches would be appropriate. The student this curriculum is for is the one whom no one knows how to teach because, as the research so clearly, persistently, and frustratedly shows, nothing seems to work with this student (Forrester, 1983; Hartwell, 1985; Hillocks, 1986; Holbrook, 1983; Kroll & Vann, 1981; Noguchi, 1991; Reynolds, 1986; Taylor, 1986). This constructivist natural human learning process approach, however, does work.

As a matter of fact, teachers should think twice about assigning journal writing for students who do not have basic grammar understanding because producing a lot of error-filled writing only reinforces whatever error-filled networks they have in their brain. What these students need is to acquire new, correct schemas. Some of my colleagues who use this curriculum do assign students to do journal and letter writing. Each teacher, of course, must do what she or he thinks best.

This approach does not have students transcribe their authentic speech into writing, as some advocate. The main reason is that informal speech and correct standard English writing are very different (Kroll & Vann, 1981; Murray, 1978). People do not speak with the scrupulous care for the formal rules that they must use when they want to produce correct writing; written sentences use combinations of dependent clauses (usually produced after much revision) which are rarely used in speaking; and as a result, writing, more than speaking, is able to capture, express, and develop complex, subtle ideas and feelings. Moreover, when writing, people have the luxury—and task—of revising to discover and develop their thoughts, an activity not characteristic of informal speech.

More important, however, our basic writing students typically do not have an ear for standard English. But their ability to write with an ear for authentic speech is not what needs to be addressed at this point in these students' writing education. What they need at this point is a firm foundation of basic grammar understanding; then they will be prepared to work on the higher-level concerns for authenticity of style and voice.

A great deal of research has been done on sentence combining. The research makes it clear that sentence combining, if it works at all, works only with students who have more grammar understanding and skill than the students for whom this curriculum is designed. In this **NHLP** curriculum, however, students work on combining their own sentences in the process of learning to use their new grammar tools.

Assumptions and Implications

1. Learning occurs when an individual actively explores and processes new material to construct his or her own new neural networks. Learners know—which means they authentically can understand and creatively, critically use—only what they have constructed neural networks for through their own personal exploration and processing. But picture this situation: A teacher is teaching at Stage 4, when lectures, demonstrations, and reading can add depth and detail to a neural network already somewhat well constructed. In the class are students who in high school or in previous courses successfully constructed relevant neural networks perhaps up to Stage 3 or 4. Thus, these students are well prepared for Stage 4. They have neural networks from which they can grow the new dendrites needed for the new concepts; at this level of dendrite growth, they literally can connect or "catch on."

In the class are also students at Stage 1 for this object of learning; they have as yet no, or only low-level, neural networks. They lack the requisite level of dendrites from which the new, higher-level dendrites, needed for the new, more sophisticated concepts, can grow; they literally cannot "catch on" or connect because the material is "above their heads" (above their dendrite levels).

In short, students who have had a good educational background are at an advantage in classes in which faculty start at Stage 4 with lectures. Students who are successful and competent in outside-school activities (or in different subjects) but who have not had a good educational background in general (or in a particular subject or for a particular object of learning) will be at a disadvantage—dendrite disadvantaged—when they are at Stage 1 and the teacher is teaching at Stage 4. They will experience the pain of cognitive drowning—and, unless they have extraordinary confidence, motivation, and perseverance, will probably drop out.

2. Human beings love to learn; it is one of the greatest sources of pleasure for our species. In fact, the brain manufactures endorphins, which produce a sensation of pleasure, when we learn. One of the brain's innate functions is to learn how the world operates, to empower the learner with knowledge of how to operate the world for the learner's own purposes and uses. As students feel their power increasing, they feel so much pleasure that they are naturally motivated.

Students learn all sorts of skills and knowledge very well outside school; however, there can be obstacles to an individual's ability to learn in an academic setting. Some of the major obstacles are incorrect and counterproductive assumptions held by students. For example, one common belief is that mistakes are bad and must be avoided. The reality, of course, is that people learn by practicing a lot, which means making and correcting sincere—not careless—mistakes and trying again and again. Another especially pernicious assumption is that, if a student cannot do a task correctly or does not understand what to do, she or he is stupid. The truth is that that student is dendrite disadvantaged from lack of prior experience and practice.

3. Students have different learning styles and preferences; thus, they might learn best when the curriculum is delivered in a varied learning environment. Such an environment might include, as in this **NHLP** approach, a combination of individual, small group, and whole group activities along with both directed practice and individual creativity.

However, students with a preference for watching and listening rather than doing have a counterproductive preference actively process their own experiences. Fear of making mistakes is often the reason learners prefer not to be active. In this curriculum, however, making mistakes is seen as necessary and important, which encourages students to take risks.

Schedule

The suggested number of fifty-minute class sessions needed for each chapter is listed below. These suggestions are for a class of basic writing students who do not know standard English grammar (for example, the elements and structures in sentences and sentence boundaries) and/or cannot use in their own writing the information they might have accumulated by rote. The skills are cumulative, each unit based on and incorporating the previous units:

1. Introduction; prewriting test; metacognitive activity and lecture (Chapter 1)...1–2 classes
2. Prepositional phrases; learning how to study grammar (Chapter 2)...4–5 classes
3. Subjects and verbs (Chapters 3, 4, 5)....................15–20 classes
4. Subject-verb completers (objects and complements); pronouns (Chapter 6)..3–4 classes
5. Independent and dependent clauses; sentences and sentence boundaries (Chapter 7)...7–10 classes
6. Relative clauses (Chapter 8)...................................5–7 classes
7. Optional: More about punctuation; modifiers; quotations; possessives (Chapter 9)...7–8 classes
8. Optional: More about word order and pronouns (Chapter 10)..2–3 classes
9. Optional: More about number and tense; person (Chapter 11)..3–6 classes
10. Optional: More about verbals for ESL students; articles; idioms (Chapter 12)..3–6 classes

As noted in the list, Chapters 9 through 12 can be used as needed: selected activities can be used as in-class work or assigned to individual students with special problems.

Homework and Tests

There is homework for every class. This homework might consist of writing more of whatever has been practiced in class. For example, students might write and analyze three sentences containing prepositional phrases or write a short essay using those structures. Students who are conscientious about studying and using all their notes and tools say writing and analyzing three sentences about a new structure or element can sometimes take an hour or more. Prompts or topics for the many homework writing assignments are in the Writing Practice section in the textbook. However, students never seem at a loss for something to write about; in fact, as their tool-use skill and understanding increase, some students become quite ambitious and write and analyze longer papers.

If, on the other hand, some students' homework is always perfect because they do not want to risk making mistakes, they might be urged to challenge themselves to write more sentences or write on more complex topics. They might be unwilling to make mistakes, but making mistakes when trying something new and more difficult is how they will learn and progress to a higher level.

Other homework topics assigned by colleagues who use this curriculum include writing responses to self-selected articles in a newspaper or news magazine, writing in journals, and writing letters to the teacher, who writes back. The colleagues who give these kinds of assignments suggest that students analyze only a short self-selected part of their journal or their letter. My view, however, is that students should not do any unanalyzed writing in this course because it will just give them more practice in, and reinforce, their nonstandard networks.

It is suggested that more formal types of writing (pretest, end-of-chapter in-class essays—which can, alternatively, be given out of class—and posttest or final exam) be responses to moral dilemmas, which not only test for the target skill of writing their own sentences but also stretch the students' critical thinking ability. Moral dilemma prompts for these in- or out-of-class essays are in this manual. These essays might also be used as tests. On the other hand, short-answer grammar tests are not useful because they do not test for students' progress toward the target skill: Although some students can get high scores on short-answer tests, this ability is not necessarily reflected in their own writing.

Suggestions for supplementary in-class writing activities for each chapter are in the Implementing the Curriculum section in this manual.

Evaluation

Evaluation of students' writing and analyses, as always, is to support, guide, facilitate, and shape students' progress. In this **NHLP** approach it is recommended that only the tools that have been learned or are in the process of being learned need to be addressed. Nothing else, no matter how egregious the error, should be noted or mentioned; all pertinent errors will be corrected in due time. For each error, it is necessary only to remind the student of the relevant tool. It is, however, imperative to write encouraging, supportive comments on every paper—even only one positive comment about one correctly analyzed word. This support is essential for developmental students who, identify at least one strength, however small, to build on. (In the Appendix to this manual are nine samples of the in-class and at-home writing of a woman in her mid-forties during an eleven-week quarter. These samples include instructor's comments.)

Feedback on Homework

It is best if the instructor evaluates all homework and returns it the following class period. This is possible because students write relatively little for each assignment and because no corrective or explanatory comments are needed on the rhetorical, compositional, or stylistic qualities of the writing. Samples of feedback on student work are in this manual.

Proofreading Practice

After students begin to acquire a schema, in the latter part of each chapter, the following alternate method for homework evaluation is rated by the students as one of the most valuable aids to their learning: In the margin, the teacher puts one check mark for each error of commission or omission in a line. (Errors, of course, are identified only for those tools already learned and currently being learned.) At the beginning of each class students might spend a few minutes working alone, then with a partner or in a small group, trying to find and correct their errors. Students with no errors work with students who have made errors.

Critical to the success of this method of evaluation and proofreading practice is the view, noted earlier, that learners—even when careful—will invariably make mistakes when learning something new, and that making and correcting these mistakes is how human beings become skillful and increase their understanding. If a student makes a sincere (not careless) mistake, he or she now has an opportunity to learn something. Also critical is the view that no one can do something she or he has not yet learned to do. That is, until a student has sufficiently processed or worked on an object of learning, the student cannot be expected to use it with skill and understanding.

In-Class Assessment

In this curriculum students are continually writing, analyzing, and handing in homework. This makes it easy for instructors to know exactly what students understand from class to class. However, it is also important for instructors to know how much students comprehend while a class session is going on. One effective method for evaluating whether the work is going too quickly or too slowly and whether students need more processing opportunities at a particular stage or are ready to go on is to draw on the board a scale from 0 to 5: 0------3-----5. Then, pointing to 0, ask the students how many of them are totally confused. (Because, in this curriculum, making mistakes and being confused are seen as normal and natural aspects of the learning process, students have no problem admitting their confusion.) Then, point to 5 and ask how many totally understand and want to go on. Then, pointing to 3, ask how many people sort of get it but not completely. If only a few students are at the lower end, you might want to have a private conference with them. This evaluation can be done several times during one class session if necessary.

Problems

Sometimes when a student asks a question or the instructor sees what a student's problem is, the temptation is to jump ahead and explain, using information not yet processed in class. However, it is imperative to focus on the tool and schema at hand and not stray away or get ahead. Straying away or jumping ahead, even when the instructor has just the right answer and just the right explanation, will result in confusion and frustration because it probably will be above the students' dendrites; thus, as noted earlier, students will not be able to catch on to the information, no matter how correct it is. In this way students' concentration, focus, and learning are not interrupted.

Another problem is that students do not intuitively grasp that sentences, to be grammatically correct, are rule-controlled. Students need to see, for example, that a correct or complete sentence, grammatically speaking (though not logically, commonsensically, or artistically speaking) needs to have only one independent subject-verb group.

One of the most problematic areas of this—and any—instructional approach is that students often don't use their new knowledge and skills outside class or in other classes. A great deal has been written by educational psychologists and educators about this problem, but no one has a definitive solution. This constructivist approach, with its constant focus on authentic processing, helps students acquire their own brain networks rather than just verbal knowledge or knowledge about a skill that is not the target skill (for example, learning to do workbook work rather than learning to do one's own writing). As a result, students in this program are more likely to use their new understanding on their own outside this course. And they do. But there is a catch: Students in this curriculum are acquiring a great deal of new complex knowledge and must expend a tremendous amount of mental energy concentrating on using their new grammar tools. Students say it can be exhausting—though they say it is also challenging, stimulating, and motivating.

Some students do not use their new knowledge and skills consistently. It is not only their cognitive effort and activities that determine whether students use their new skills and knowledge; their emotional, motivational, and habitual responses also play a critical role. For example, some students have poor study and work habits; some students seem content with low-level performance and do not challenge themselves to reach a higher level. There are also some students who do not want to risk making mistakes. Some of the hardest cases are ESL students who have become "fossilized" at a level of achievement with which they have been able to get by and do not want to leave that level of comfort and start over again with a different method, going from feeling competent to feeling incompetent. Most of these students respond to constant, positive support and praise—and, when necessary, with honest confrontation—but always in a way that shows the teacher's unswerving belief in their intelligence and their ability to succeed. Some students' problems, however, are beyond an instructor's expertise and a particular student might need to be referred to a counselor or advisor.

Implementing the Curriculum

The next part of this manual contains suggestions for teaching the curriculum by the **Natural Human Learning Process** approach. The section for Chapter 1 provides additional information to support the teaching of the first chapter in the textbook. The beginning of the section for Chapter 2 gives a detailed introduction to the **NHLP** instructional approach. At the end of each section are answers to questions teachers have asked about the chapter. The comments also include troubleshooting suggestions and pointers.

IMPLEMENTING THE CURRICULUM

IM Chapters for Chapters 1 to 12

CHAPTER 1

WHAT YOU NEED TO KNOW
BEFORE YOU GET STARTED

The content of this chapter can be the topic of the first few sessions of the course—but no more than that because students have a great many grammar concepts and skills to learn, and the sooner they begin working on them, the better.

The First-Day Handout (Syllabus)

Here is an example of a syllabus to hand out on the first day of class. It emphasizes confidence in the students' intelligence and in their ability to be successful students.

COURSE SYLLABUS
WRITING CORRECT SENTENCES

TEXTBOOKS: Tools for Writing (Using the Natural Human Learning Process) Any dictionary

COURSE OBJECTIVES:

By the end of the quarter you will be able to express your ideas in writing in grammatically correct sentences—and you will know exactly how to do that.

You will gain confidence as a writer.

You will also improve your college-level speaking, listening, and thinking skills.

REQUIREMENTS:

1. You are required to do all in-class and homework assignments.
2. You will need to keep a file of all the work that I evaluate and return to you. This file must be turned in at the end of the quarter for you to receive credit for the course. Put your name and the date on every assignment that you hand in.
3. There will be writing practice to do at home for every class. Unless otherwise stated, for this writing practice you will write three to five sentences or a short paragraph using the tools you were working on in class. The book has a list of suggested topics to write about (see pages 440 to 442).

ATTENDANCE:

Much of the learning will go on through discussion and group work in class, so being in class is absolutely essential. Also, learning is a step-by-step process. If you miss one step, you will find it difficult to keep up and progress. Therefore, attending class should be your first priority.

The Pretest

It is important to give a pretest as soon as possible, preferably during the first class session, both to be sure the students have been correctly placed and also to provide a baseline to be contrasted to a posttest. This is one method by which you can later assess the students' progress and the course's effectiveness.

Moral dilemmas are suggested as prompts for the pretest and also for the weekly in-class essays because this kind of prompt invites students to do higher-level, complex thinking. Far from being intimidated by these prompts, students are motivated and stimulated by them. In fact, one of the main benefits is that the students feel that their intelligence and their knowledge of life are respected to be given such a challenging task. This in itself is powerfully motivating. Moreover, as they proceed through the course, they become more and more empowered to express their complex ideas and feelings in correct sentences.

Another benefit of using this type of prompt is that students are also practicing their reading skills. To respond to these assignments they must relate the words on the page to what they know of reality; this is essential for good reading comprehension.

The suggested writing pretest (see following) is an especially complex dilemma (adapted from Kohlberg). It stretches students to do complex thinking, militating against their writing only simple sentences—which they might be able to control—and thus hiding their true lack of sentence-grammar knowledge. But when they are challenged by a complex prompt, they are impelled by the complexity of their thoughts to use complex structures to express these complex thoughts. This brings out the true level of their sentence knowledge (Smilkstein, 1994).

For this writing pretest, hand out a copy of a challenging prompt, such as the one following. Read it aloud, making sure they understand the vocabulary, the content, and what their task is. The students then write for fifteen to twenty minutes, double-spacing.

PRETEST: PART 1

A woman was near death from a special kind of cancer. There was one new drug that the doctors thought might save her. The drug had recently been discovered by a scientist who lived in the same city, and it had already saved several other cancer patients who were close to death. The scientist refused to sell his formula to a drug company or even to share it with other scientists. He was charging ten times what it cost him to make the drug. He paid two hundred dollars for the ingredients and charged customers two thousand dollars for it. The dying woman's husband Bill, a poor retired janitor, went, to everyone he knew to borrow the money, but he could get only one thousand dollars. The couple had no children, and they were each other's only family. Bill told the scientist that his wife was dying and asked whether he could pay less or pay the rest later. But the scientist said, "I worked very hard and at great personal sacrifice for twenty years to discover this drug. My family also sacrificed for all those years while I worked night and day on my research, and my wife had to work to support us. If I let you have it cheaper, I will have to let everyone have it cheaper. This isn't fair to my own wife and children. I'm sorry." Bill got desperate and broke into the scientist's laboratory to steal the drug for his wife. He got caught and was arrested.

Your Task: You are a member of the jury deciding Bill's case. You need to decide whether Bill is guilty or not and, if you think he is guilty, what his punishment should be. What is your decision on these questions: Is Bill guilty or not? Why do you think this? And if you think he is guilty, what should his punishment be? Why should it be that?

When the time is up, even if students have not finished their writing, hand out the analysis direction sheet that follows, read through it with them, and then give them ten to fifteen minutes to analyze the response they have just written.

PRETEST: PART 2

To be sure you are in the right class, please identify the following elements in what you have just written. If you cannot identify these, you are in the right class. By the end of the course you will confidently be able to do this, and you will know how to express your ideas and feelings in sentences with correct grammar. On the other hand, if you can identify these elements, and if your writing is at a high enough level, I will recommend that you take a higher-level course.

1. Put parentheses around all your **prepositional phrases**, for example,

Jane went (to the library) after Liu left.

2. Put one line under all your **subjects,** for example,

<u>Jane</u> went (to the library) after <u>Liu</u> left.

3. Put two lines under all your **verbs**, for example,

<u>Jane</u> <u>went</u> (to the library) after <u>Liu</u> <u>left</u>.

4. Draw a line between every **subject** and its verb; for example,

<u>Jane</u> <u>went</u> (to the library) after <u>Liu</u> <u>left</u>.

5. Put a wavy line under all your **dependent clauses,** for example,

<u>Jane</u> <u>went</u> (to the library) after <u>Liu</u> <u>left</u>.

∧∧∧∧∧∧∧∧∧

Presenting the Material

If your class meets more than three times a week in a semester or five times a week in a quarter, you might assign students to read the whole chapter. If you decide to include the summary-writing activity, which is a critical thinking activity, it is important to provide time during the next class session for students to share their work in small groups and then as a whole class. This type of small group–whole class interaction immediately begins to create a class community. If your class meets less often, you might, instead, prefer to summarize the chapter and then assign the students to read only a few selected sections. However, whether you choose to summarize the chapter yourself or to assign the students to read all or parts of it, it is essential to focus on the sections about how the brain learns ("How the Brain Learns," "Emotions Make a Difference," "Why It Is That Sometimes People Don't Learn," "We Learn What We Practice," and "How the Brain and the Natural Human Learning Process Work Together"). The information in these sections is essential because it introduces the brain's **Natural Human Learning Process.** Understanding this process provides students with the metacognitive knowledge they need to be empowered as learners. An article in this manual walks you through the metacognitive activity on page 8 in the textbook, explaining how to present and use it.

For example, students will see that they learn only when structures in their brain grow and that only they can grow the structures in their own brain through their own effort. As a result, they see that they are responsible for their own learning and, moreover, that they must be active learners. This metacognitive knowledge never fails to increase student motivation. Students will now also have concepts and terms for talking about and evaluating their learning.

To help you present this material to your students, this manual provides further information (pages 10–11). You might want to make overheads of figures on pages 5 to 6 in the textbook as an additional aid to class discussion, especially if the students aren't assigned to read and discuss the chapter.

After these orientation activities, students can begin work on Chapter 2, the first content chapter.

The Natural Human Learning Process, Learning Styles, and the Curriculum

No matter what a person's learning style or preference is, his or her brain learns by the same innate learning process: personal practice through increasing levels of complexity, refinement, and sophistication causes physical structures in the learner's brain to grow and to connect in networks of ever-increasing complexity *for the specific skill or concept being practiced.* The growth of these physical networks *is* learning: as these networks grow and connect, the learner's skill and understanding increases. Moreover, the learner has the conscious awareness of learning.

Thus, the curriculum needs to provide practice (learning) opportunities from a low level of complexity, sophistication, and refinement to higher and higher levels for each specific concept or skill (schema) so that the appropriate brain structures will grow and connect in more and more complex networks. The curriculum in this book presents such practice opportunities.

This curriculum begins with the expectation that developmental students at this beginning level lack brain networks (experienced as a lack of knowledge and skill) for recognizing and/or controlling sentence elements and structures (such as **subjects [S], verbs [V], and clauses**) in their own sentences. This curriculum, then, provides learning opportunities at a naive, unrefined level for each sentence element and structure so that students can construct foundational networks. The curriculum, then, provides opportunities for students to construct cumulatively more and more complex, refined, and sophisticated networks.

But how do we know which concept, which sentence element, to start with and then which one to proceed to? We begin by identifying the outcome we want for the students. The outcome identified in this book is that students will be able to express their thoughts and feelings in correct sentences and know exactly how to do that. Then we need to ask what they need to know in order to do that. They need to know what **independent clauses (IC)** are. But what do they need to know in order to know that? They need to know what **subjects (S)** and **verbs (V)** are. But because students at this level often mistake **objects of prepositions (OP)** for **subjects (S)**, they need to start by learning what **prepositional phrases (PP)** are.

There is an additional advantage to starting with **prepositional phrases (PP)**: they are a simpler sentence structure than **clauses**. By starting with this clear-cut and relatively simple structure, students have the opportunity not only to acquire the concept of—and skill at identifying and using—this structure, but also to begin learning how to learn about grammar. That is, they begin learning about the importance of being precise and careful and the need to practice, practice, practice.

The book is organized in five sections:

Chapter 1:	Introduction
Chapters 2–6:	Foundation (**prepositional phrases [PP], subjects [S], verbs [V], compounds**)
Chapters 7–8:	Major Structures (**clauses, sentences, sentence boundary errors**)
Chapters 9–11:	Additional material to be used whenever a whole chapter or part of a chapter is appropriate for a teacher's goals and his or her students' needs
Chapter 12 (for ESL students):	Additional material to be used whenever the whole chapter or part of the chapter is appropriate for the teacher's goals and his or her ESL students' needs

Figure 1.1

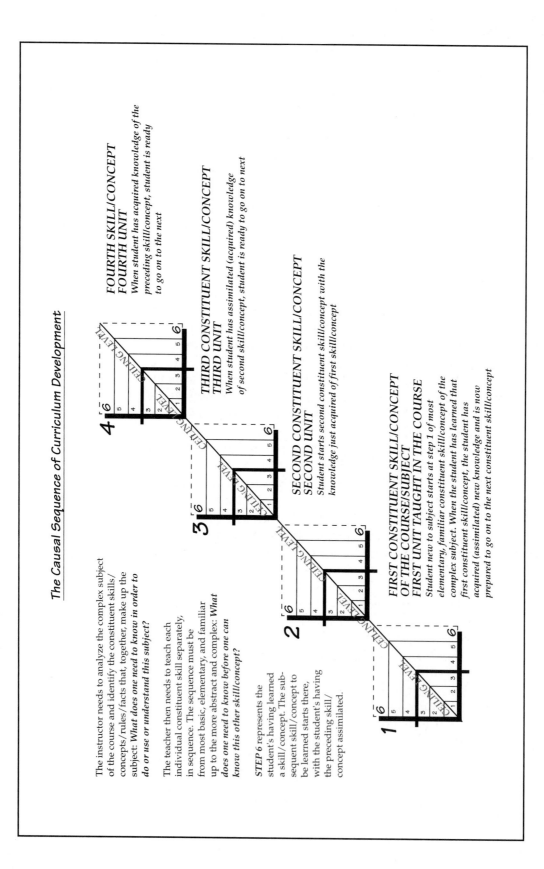

The Causal Sequence of Curriculum Development

The instructor needs to analyze the complex subject of the course and identify the constituent skills/concepts/rules/facts that, together, make up the subject: *What does one need to know in order to do or use or understand this subject?*

The teacher then needs to teach each individual constituent skill separately, in sequence. The sequence must be from most basic, elementary, and familiar up to the more abstract and complex: *What does one need to know before one can know this other skill/concept?*

STEP 6 represents the student's having learned a skill/concept. The subsequent skill/concept to be learned starts there, with the student's having the preceding skill/concept assimilated.

FOURTH SKILL/CONCEPT
FOURTH UNIT
When student has acquired knowledge of the preceding skill/concept, student is ready to go on to the next

THIRD CONSTITUENT SKILL/CONCEPT
THIRD UNIT
When student has assimilated (acquired) knowledge of second skill/concept, student is ready to go on to next

SECOND CONSTITUENT SKILL/CONCEPT
SECOND UNIT
Student starts second constituent skill/concept with the knowledge just acquired of first skill/concept

FIRST CONSTITUENT SKILL/CONCEPT
OF THE COURSE/SUBJECT
FIRST UNIT TAUGHT IN THE COURSE
Student new to subject starts at step 1 of most elementary, familiar constituent skill/concept of the complex subject. When the student has learned that first constituent skill/concept, the student has acquired (assimilated) new knowledge and is now prepared to go on to the next constituent skill/concept

A primary objective is to complete Chapters 2 through 8 in approximately 35 hours and, without shortchanging the concepts and skills in Chapters 2 to 6, to provide as much time as possible for students to work on the concepts and skills in Chapters 7 and 8, the two core or culminating chapters (**clauses** and **sentences**).

This curriculum is based on the expectation that with enough cumulative, appropriately sequenced skills and concepts, every student whose brain is not impaired will be able to construct the complex brain networks underlying sophisticated, complex, refined knowledge and skill. It is important to have this expectation because, as research shows, teachers' expectations about their students have a powerful effect on how well their students succeed. For example, Hull, Rose, Fraser, and Castellano (1991), reviewing the history of developmental education in America, conclude that low-achieving students have been, and still are, seen and treated "as if they were lesser in character and fundamental ability" (page 311). In their analysis of classroom discourse, they found that teachers' deeply ingrained and tacit assumptions about their students' abilities are the key to how teachers "structure a course and circumscribe the learning that students will do in it. . . . [We], as teachers, can inadvertently participate in the social construction of attitudes and beliefs about remediation which may limit the learning that takes place in our classrooms" (page 300).

Even though everyone has the same brain-based natural learning process, some people learn more easily through seeing while others learn more easily through hearing. (Everyone learns through hands-on or kinesthetic experience, though some people prefer not to try something new on their own.) Moreover, people have different tastes and preferences; thus, different people are more comfortable in or prefer different learning environments and situations. For these reasons, students need to have a variety of learning modalities and methods available to them. This book provides a variety of such modalities and methods: there are both words and pictures; students work alone, in small groups, and as a whole class; students copy the rules (tools) the teacher writes on the board or shows on an overhead as she or he reads them aloud. The book also has the tools printed in a more detailed form for students to read and study out of class; the analysis of sentences used in this book has both letter codes (for example, **V** for **verb**) and visual symbols (for example, square brackets around **dependent clauses [DC]**); students write and **analyze** their own sentences, but there are also models as examples. By experiencing this variety of modalities, students are able to work from their strengths as well as to increase their repertoire of learning strategies.

The mottos of this curriculum are 1) practice, practice, practice the actual skills and concepts that are targeted because brain networks grow, tailor-made, for what is being practiced; 2) thoroughness in constructing foundations is infinitely more important than covering material; 3) all students are smart, want to learn, and enjoy learning—when they can learn by their brain's innate learning process.

Writing Essays

As discussed in Chapter 1, there is not enough time in one term for students to construct the firm and thorough knowledge and skill needed for expressing their own ideas and feelings in correct sentences and also to learn the extremely complex skill of how to write an essay. However, although the focus of this book is to help students gain control over their sentences, students do a great deal of writing: sentence and/or paragraph writing homework, as well as in-class essays. Because the in-class essay assignments can be given as tests, moral dilemma prompts for these assignments are in this *Instructor's Manual* rather than in the textbook itself. The "Writing Practice" section at the end of the textbook provides topics for out-of-class (homework) writing. The first level of these topics is suitable for the recommended three to five sentences to be written and **analyzed** as out-of-class homework for each class. The second level of topics is suitable for writing paragraphs. Each instructor will need to use his or her judgment about how much of the writing work will be appropriate for his or her students and course.

Interesting Problems to Solve

Each chapter includes a section of sentences for students to **analyze**. These sentences are intended to give students the option of doing further thinking about the concepts, codes, and symbols they are learning. **Analyzing** these sentences is not intended to replace the learning activities of their doing—and **analyzing**—their own writing and is not intended to be done in class, taking up valuable class time. Answers are provided at the end of each chapter so that students can check and correct their work.

Because we know that transfer from workbook activities to the students' own writing does not occur, and because doing their own writing is the goal of the course, what the students most need to practice and work on is their own writing. Thus, when students work on these "interesting problems," we cannot expect that this will improve their own writing. It can provide only some support for students whose learning preference is to study models or congenial work for students who enjoy analytical work and problem-solving.

If students work on these problems, they should be directed to read the analyses ("solutions") at the end of the chapter and to check and correct each sentence as they do it. In this way they can learn more about what they are doing as they continue.

It is important for students to know that in this one course there just isn't time to learn every grammar tool (rule) for writing sentences. This is because the sentence is one of the most complex structures human beings have ever created. But students in this course will construct a firm foundation of concepts and skills for the tools that are the most important for writing correct sentences. With this foundation, they will find it easier in their later English courses to learn whatever else they did not have time to study in this course.

PREPOSITIONAL PHRASES

This manual on pages 26 to 29 discusses the organization of each chapter as well as the key elements in this brain-based, **Natural Human Learning Process** approach. These key elements are implemented in the activities that characterize this approach:

1. Sequences of **individual, small group, whole class** activities
2. Sufficient practice opportunities for students to increase their understanding, skill, and fluency
3. **Critical thinking activities** whenever possible before a new tool is introduced: in these activities, students try to solve problems that are just above their **ceiling level** and that anticipate the new tool to be introduced. These activities not only give students an opportunity to review and process the tools they have learned up to that point, but they also provide the brain with the stimulus it needs to prepare for learning. Moreover, students enjoy the challenge because risk-taking errors are not punished. Finding the correct answer is *not* important. What *is* important is that students do critical mental processing that reaches to the limits of, and stretches, their present knowledge and skill. As a result, students are ready and eager to learn the new tool.

Students learn through practice; thus, it is essential that students also do out-of-class writing (homework) to hand in at each class session for evaluation and feedback. As stated on the sample course syllabus (page 23), "There will be writing practice to do at home for every class. Unless otherwise stated, for this writing practice you will write three to five sentences or a short paragraph using the tools you were working on in class." Because it is more difficult to write paragraphs than sentences, each teacher will need to decide the level of difficulty best for his or her students, perhaps not assigning paragraphs until Chapter 7.

These activities are described here for Chapter 2 in greater detail than in later chapters. The detailed descriptions here are meant to serve as a template for the activities in the other chapters.

Review, page 16

Individual: Each student writes his or her own answer for a few minutes. This provides the opportunity for students to process using their own "mind store" of knowledge, experience, and understanding (stimulating their **dendrites** and **neural networks**).

Small Group: Students join with several neighbors to share their ideas. This provides the opportunity for interactivity, comparing and contrasting perspectives, and peer tutoring, which, research shows, is a powerful learning situation for both the tutor and the tutee. (As the teacher circulates and listens in, he or she can check to see how many groups are finished. When several groups are finished, students can proceed to the next step.)

Whole Class: Students come back together as a whole group and share their ideas with others in the class. The teacher might want to write their ideas on the board and advise students to copy the information into their notebook.

Note: When the teacher writes students' responses on the board, it is important to write them verbatim. This gives students the message that their ideas are valued. Instead of the teacher commenting on student responses, students might be invited to say whether they agree or disagree with others' responses. If there is a disagreement—or if no one sees a mistake—the teacher might ask the class to research the point in Chapter 1. This approach begins the essential work of creating a community of learners doing critical thinking in a supportive, collaborative environment.

Knowledge Evaluation, page 17

These self-evaluation activities are an essential element in students' **metacognitive** development, that is, in their learning about and being aware of their own learning processes. With **metacognitive** awareness, students realize they are responsible for their own learning. It is especially important to this end that students connect their own efforts with the growing of structures in their own brain and understand that this brain growth is learning. By making this connection, students can see they are the only ones who can grow their own brain's structures, that is, that they are the only ones who can make themselves learn.

To introduce students to this **metacognitive** self-evaluation activity, which is repeated in every chapter, it would help if the teacher were to draw the first diagram on the board and model its use, explaining and showing that those students who don't know anything about **prepositions (P)** should put their "X" at the bottom. If they know them very well, they are to put their "X" at the top. If they know something about **prepositions (P)** but aren't completely confident, they are to put their "X" somewhere in the middle, wherever it feels right to each individual.

Individual: Students do the first evaluation.
Small Group: Students share and discuss their evaluations.
Whole Class: Students debrief by discussing their **individual** and **small group** experiences and by asking questions.

After being introduced to this self-evaluation method, students will be able to do it on their own. After Chapter 2 it is up to each teacher to decide if and how much class time will be spent on it or whether it should be done for homework.

Additional Evaluation, page 17

An evaluation method especially useful for visual learners is one in which students are given a page with "brain cell bodies" on it (or draw their own). Then they draw on these cell bodies the number and length of **dendrites** they think they have for the concepts in the previous chapter and explain why they think they have that amount of **dendrites**. This evaluation method is then also used as the pre-evaluation for the concepts in the new chapter. See examples in Chapter 2. If a teacher wants to use this evaluation instrument, he or she might choose to reproduce the following picture for students to use or might ask students to draw their own cell bodies following the examples on page 18. This picture is also in the "Transparency Masters" section in the back of this manual.

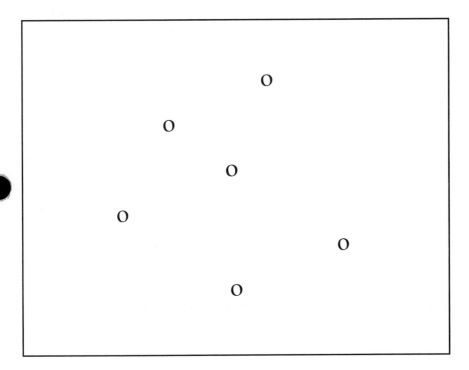

Classwork 2-1, page 19

If from the pretest and their first self-evaluation it is clear that some students can readily identify the **prepositions (P)** in their own writing, it will be important to explain that some students might find this chapter easy if their **ceiling level** (see Chapter 1) is high for **prepositions (P)**. They can be assured, however, that the work will get more difficult and challenging as they go on to later chapters. The teacher might want to invite them to do extra-credit writing assignments (some of the assignments in the essay list of the "Writing Practice" section) if they want more challenging assignments in the meantime.

Individual: Students do the first activity (write their answer to "Where is this person?" on page 19). It is essential to remind students that they learn (their **dendrites** grow) when they are active learners.

Small Group: When the majority have finished the **individual** work, they should check with a few neighbors to see whether they all have done the activity correctly. As the work gets more challenging and complex, they will have more comparing, contrasting, and discussing to do in their **small groups** as they help each other understand the tools and correct their use of the tools in their work.

Whole Class: The debriefing at the end of the **small group** interaction can start with the question, "What did you come up with?" Then the teacher writes their responses on the board, as in the examples following:

> in the box
> inside the cube

If, however, a student says something like "standing in the box," the students need to be reminded of the exact task and the need to be precise and careful. Being precise and careful will be two of the students' most important aids for learning—and two of their most difficult challenges.

The teacher might ask, "Does this answer '*Where* is this person?' Remember, this was the question."

Note: After any question the teacher asks, it helps students if the teacher waits for students to answer, even if it takes some time.

Then, the teacher might ask, "What *does* it answer?" If no one answers, the teacher can supply the answer: "*What* is this person doing?"

The students must understand it is essential that they always answer the exact question in order to learn these complex sentence-writing tools.

After several of their contributions have been written on the board, the teacher can write a list of **prepositions (P)** on the board, using the words the students have contributed, as in this example:

> **Preposition List**
> in
> inside

Students should write this list on page 39. As they continue doing their classwork, they will add new **prepositions (P)** to this list. They also need to be informed that there is a list of **prepositions (P)** in the book on page 44–45 but that it is always good for them to start learning something new by first writing it in their own handwriting because their own physical activity helps begin the growing and connecting of their **dendrites**.

When a student offers a nonpreposition, this second list should be started on the board. Students are to copy the list, as in this example:

> **Never-a-Preposition List**
> the
> a
> standing

At this stage in their learning, when they have no mental concept of what a **preposition (P)** is and are starting to construct a mental concept of it, the **"Never-a-Preposition List"** is as important as the **"Preposition List."** The teacher might add to this list at the start of each class, using mistakes from their homework.

The teacher can now introduce **Tool 1**. All tools should be written on the board or presented on an overhead projector for students to copy in their book. All the tools are in the "Transparency Masters" section in the back of this manual.

It is more effective for student learning to introduce tools after students have done some preliminary processing on their own and talked about it with each other. This preprocessing of experimenting and exploring on their own stimulates their brain to grow and connect **dendrites** (learn). When the learning situation is supportive and mistakes are seen as part of the learning process, learners find this kind of challenge to be fun, like an interesting problem-solving game.

TOOL 1: Prepositions (P) are on the "Preposition List." They are *never* **on the "Never-a-Preposition List."**

The second part of this tool might seem unnecessary; but for insecure, anxious, unprepared students this kind of absolutely dependable and clear tool is what they need to begin building a sense of confidence, competence, and control. It gives them a firm handle or tool to hold onto for security. We cannot overestimate the degree of anxiety that some of these students might be feeling. This tool, however, makes them feel, "This is at my level. I can do this." They find **Tool 1** reassuring. They need to be reassured that when they use these—and all the other **preposition (P)** tools—they will be able to recognize **prepositions (P)** in their own sentences.

After being introduced to **Tool 1**, students are now to go back to their answer to "Where is this person?" and **individually analyze** what they wrote by putting a **P** over their **preposition**. Then they are to check with one or two neighbors in a **small group** to see whether they all **analyzed** their work correctly. It is always helpful after the **individual** and **small group** work to ask the **whole class** whether there are any questions or problems.

After the **whole class** debriefing at the end of the first activity of Classwork 2-1 (page 20), they will be ready for **Tools 2-5**. These can be introduced one after the other with illustrative examples for each one.

TOOL 2: Prepositions (P) can *never* **have "a," "an," or "the" in front of them, if necessary.**

TOOL 3: Ask "what?" or "whom?" *after* **a preposition (P). If there is an answer, the answer is the object of the preposition (OP). If there is no answer (no OP), then there is no preposition (no P). Use your own logic to decide what the answer is.**

Students now will need the opportunity to practice using their sense of logic to find the whole answer to the question "what?" or "whom?" after the **preposition (P)**.

The **prepositional phrases (PP)** on the board from Classwork 2-1 can be used for practice; for example, "Ask 'what?' or 'whom?' after 'in.' Is there an answer?" When students say there is—and they will—the next question is, "What is the *whole* answer?" Students will also be able to answer this question by using their innate sense of logic.

This should be repeated with one or two more of their **prepositional phrases (PP)** on the board. They will improve their fluency at seeing the whole answer the more they practice. Having a highly developed ability to see whole structures and units of thought is critical to gaining control over the sentence.

Students should then **individually analyze** their own answer from Classwork 2-1 by putting —OP— over their whole **object of the preposition (OP)**. After this, as usual, they should look at and help each other correct their analyses in **small groups**. Finally, calling them together again as a **whole class**, the teacher can put more of their work on the board and invite their questions.

It is very important that students learn to recognize when there is no answer to "what?" or "whom?" after the **preposition (P)**—and, thus, no **object of the preposition (OP)** or **preposition (P)** (**Tool 3**). To learn this they will need further practice opportunities. For example, the teacher might write a pair of illustrative examples on the board (always without the analysis) and have the class **analyze** them **individually**, in **small groups**, and as a **whole class (I-SG-WC)**; for example, "It is inside the box" and "He went inside."

Analysis   inside what?   **Analysis   inside what?**
        P   ^ ---OP---   P?   ^
    It is inside ^ the box.   He went inside.

During **whole class** debriefing, students should identify what the whole answer to "what?" is for each **preposition (P)**. If students want to know what the second "inside" is and how to analyze it, an effective response is to let them know that they will learn about it later and that, if they don't know what a word is, they should leave it alone and not analyze it.

After students **analyze** "He went inside," the teacher might ask students to make "inside" a **preposition (P)** (add an **object of the preposition [OP]**) **I-SG-WC**. During the **whole class** debriefing, volunteers (or the teacher) can put some of their work on the board, for example,

inside what?
        P   ----OP----
    He went inside ^ the house.

If students feel they need more practice, this activity can be repeated with another pair of sentences. It is helpful to call these sentences "problems" or "brain teasers" and to ask the students to try to "solve" the problems, for example,

They ran down the hill.   She laid it down.

Note: The questions "what?" and "whom?"—as well as all the analysis codes (for example, **P** and **OP**)—are used as **scaffolding** to support students as they begin, shakily at first, to grow their new **dendrites, synapses,** and **neural networks**. The codes and tools give the students something concrete and logical to hold onto and use. This makes it possible for them to develop their confidence, competence, and control.

It is important for them to use the scaffolding of analysis codes and symbols (like parentheses around **prepositional phrases [PP]**) as meticulously as possible in order to construct their complex new **neural networks**. Later, as students gain skill and fluency, the codes can begin to be eliminated in their analyses. For example, after becoming fluent at identifying **prepositions (P), objects of prepositions (OP)** and, later, **prepositional phrases (PP)**, they can **analyze** them with just the symbol of the parentheses and eliminate all the codes:

At the beginning of learning new element or structure:

After being able to identify a the new element or structure:

———PP———-
P ——OP——
(in the classroom)

(in the classroom)

Using abbreviations in class discussions of the tools and analyses (actually saying **"prep," "P,"** and **"OP"**) helps the students increase their comfort and fluency with the coding and the grammatical elements and structures in the sentence. It becomes a well-known and well-understood language for them.

Tool 4: This is one of the most important tools. What a word is in a sentence depends on how it is used in that sentence.

To illustrate each tool, the teacher can write sentences (without analysis) on the board for students to copy and **analyze** in their book, **I-SG-WC**. The examples and discussion here should focus on and reinforce **Tools 3 and 4.**

outside what?
P? Not a P   P   ▲—OP—
She put the cat outside.   She put the cat outside the house.

Tool 5: The object of the preposition (OP) stops at the end of the *whole* **answer to "what?" or "whom?" asked after the preposition (P). Use your logic to know where the object of the preposition (OP) stops.**

This tool will be not be clear to students at first. They will need to be reminded frequently to read along through the sentence until they come to the end of the answer to "what?" or "whom?" after the **preposition (P)**. They need to recognize they can rely on their sense of logic to know what the end of the answer is. Further, they need to view their sense of logic as one of their greatest resources. Practice at finding the whole answer will soon prove to them just how strong their sense of logic is.

The teacher can write sample sentences on the board for students to practice **analyzing** as before. As always, for maximum brain stimulation the work is best done in the three-step sequence of **I-SG-WC**.

around what?

P   ▲————————OP—————————

She walked around | the large, deep, blue lake.

around what?

P   ▲——OP——

She walked around | the yard yesterday.

around what? (no OP, so no P) This point is essential.

P?   ▲

She walked around | all night.

As part of the **whole class** discussion, students can be asked what question "yesterday" and "all night" answer ("when?"). It must be stressed that "when?" is not in **Tool 3** and that they must use the tools exactly. Students should also be reminded to use all their tools.

Students will need to have it reinforced that, if they don't know what a word is, they should leave it alone and not **analyze** it. This is because there isn't enough time in this one course to learn all the different kinds of words in a sentence. In this course they will be learning only the kinds of words that are most important for learning how to write their ideas in sentences with correct grammar.

Note: Students should use the coding format exactly and **analyze** for now only on top of the sentence because later they will be **analyzing** underneath as well. To learn this complicated subject they need to be careful and to follow directions precisely at all times.

Classwork 2-1, page 21

After the **whole class** debriefing, students will be ready for **Tool 6**, the last tool needed for constructing a clear and complete concept of **prepositions (P)** and **objects of prepositions (OP)**. Now that students have some knowledge of what these elements are, students can begin their introduction to **Tool 6** with a problem to solve, writing it in their book and trying to **analyze** it **I-SG-WC**. Students will benefit from exploring and experimenting on their own as they try to solve this problem using the tools they have been learning. This is a **critical thinking** activity that stimulates their brain to get ready to learn more.

up above what?

P   P   ▲——OP——

It is up above | the desk right now.

Tool 6: There can be two prepositions (P) in a row. Ask "what?" or "whom?" after both together.

To give students the opportunity to practice and to increase their fluency, another example or two can be given for them to copy in their book and to **analyze I-SG-WC**, for example,

down under what?

P   P ▲—OP—
The ship is down under| the sea.

Note: Throughout this manual, examples are given with their **analysis.** However, these or the teacher's own examples should, of course, always be presented to the students as unanalyzed "problems" for them to solve (**analyze**) **I-SG-WC**.

To complete the introduction to **prepositions (P)**, students need an example to introduce them to the **idioms** on the list, for example, "out of" or "on top of." The teacher can point out the **idiom** "on top of" on the list of **prepositions (P)** and define **"idiom";** for example, "Idioms are ways of using words that have no rules. They must be memorized." Here are examples of some "problems" the teacher might write on the board for students to solve **I-SG-WC** in one of two equally correct ways, as they prefer:

——P—— —OP—   P OP   P —OP—
(on top of the desk)   (on top)⟍ (of the desk)

After the **whole class** debriefing at the end of this activity, a problem might be given for students to solve **I-SG-WC**—as a review and as one more opportunity to practice and increase their fluency— before they are introduced to **Tool 7**, for example,

P   —————————OP—————
They drove around the sharp, dangerous curve.

Tool 7: A prepositional phrase (PP) is two or more words that logically go together. It starts with a P and ends with an OP. Use your own logic to know which words go together.

Whatever problem was on the board for the previous activity can be used now to illustrate **Tool 7**, for example,

(—————————PP—————————)
P —————————OP—————
(around the sharp, dangerous curve)

After the **whole class (WC)** debriefing, the teacher can provide a **critical thinking** challenge for students to copy in their book and to **analyze I-SG-WC;** for example, "With a quick, intelligent remark the student in the advanced math class showed she had a talent for even the most complex math concepts."

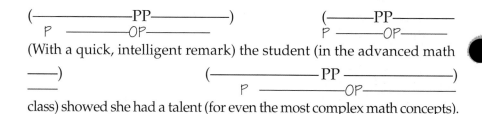

(With a quick, intelligent remark) the student (in the advanced math class) showed she had a talent (for even the most complex math concepts).

Students are stimulated and delighted by this kind of complex and challenging problem. It stretches their mind as they concentrate hard and do a lot of **critical thinking**—using their tools, growing and connecting more and more **dendrites**. This activity will also help students increase their fluency.

Because it takes a long time to construct new **neural networks** for these sentence structures—and even seemingly simple structures are difficult for students who come to the course with few or no sentence-structure **neural networks**—students will still need practice and reminders to ask "what?" or "whom?" after the **preposition (P)**. They will need to be reminded to end the **prepositional phrase (PP)** at the end of the **object of the preposition (OP)**. They will need to be reminded and guided to read through the **sentence** until they come to the end of the answer to "what?" or "whom?" after the **preposition (P)** to find the end of the **object of the preposition (OP)** and, thus, the end of the **prepositional phrase (PP)**. Teachers will probably find that they will need to write comments like "Be careful" and "Use your tools" on students' homework a lot, too. However, it encourages and motivates students when teachers also write at least one positive and encouraging comment on each paper.

But the motto is, "Practice, practice, practice!" With sufficient practice, students will construct their new **neural networks**, becoming skillful and fluent at identifying **prepositional phrases (PP)** in their own sentences.

Classwork 2-1, page 23

After the **whole class** debriefing, write a sample on the board to prepare students for **Tool 8;** for example, "The pen is inside the box on the desk."

They will need to use all their tools to solve this problem.

(—— PP ——) (——PP——)
P   —OP—   P —OP—
The pen is (inside the box) (on the desk).

As students gain understanding, skill, and fluency, they can begin to eliminate some of the scaffolding. The teacher can show students how to **analyze** using less of the codes, for example,

The pen is (inside the box) (on the desk).

Tool 8: If there are two or more PP's in a row, you can analyze them as separate PP's or you can analyze them as going together. Do it the way that is most logical for you.

—————————PP—————   or

———PP——   ———PP———   —————————— PP ——————————

(inside the box) (on the desk)   (inside the box on the desk)

—————————PP—————

———PP——

or   (inside the box (on the desk))

The teacher can point out that all three ways are correct, that each student should do it the way that seems most logical to him or her—as long as he or she uses all the tools.

The teacher might write another problem on the board for the students to solve, stressing that there are different correct ways to **analyze** these sentences and that each person has his or her own sense of logic; for example, She is in the room down the hall at her home.

(———PP——) (——— PP———) (—— PP ——)

She is (in the room) (down the hall) (at her home).

Or, if they see the whole series of **phrases** as the whole answer to "what?" or "whom?" after the **preposition (P),** they can put them together as one long **prepositional phrase (PP).**

(—————————PP—————————)

(in the room down the hall at her home)

or they might see some **phrases (PP)** as subsets of others:

(—————————PP—————————)

(———————PP———————)

(——PP——)

(in the room (down the hall (at her home)))

The teacher can give students a sample **sentence** like this to copy and **analyze:**

(———PP———)

I want (to buy a new car).

If a teacher has students who know what **infinitives (Inf)** are, he or she can introduce **Tool 9.** Otherwise, he or she can wait until Chapter 4 when the class studies this type of **verbal (Vbl).** At that time the teacher can explain **infinitives (Inf)** at the **ceiling level** the class will have by then.

Tool 9: If you know what infinitives (Inf) are, you may analyze them as infinitives (Inf) or as prepositional phrases (PP). (We will study infinitives [Inf] in Chapter 4.)

Note: At the beginning, because students know very little about grammar, some of the concepts must necessarily remain incomplete. For example, because students don't understand yet what **subjects (S), verbs (V),** and **verbals (Vbl)** are, it is premature, confusing, and counterproductive to make distinctions between **prepositional phrases (PP), infinitives (Inf),** and **dependent clauses (DC).** At this early stage, such distinctions can only be memorized by rote.

Instead, it is more important for students to construct a firm foundation at their level of understanding. Having this kind of foundation gives students confidence and motivation. Then, upon this solid foundation new, more refined, more complex, in-depth, and sophisticated understanding is later constructed—with confidence—in a connected, cumulative sequence. And the mistakes that students make as a result of any initial incomplete and lower-level understanding are easily corrected later as students' understanding develops and increases.

More specifically, it is of no importance for the purpose of writing grammatically correct sentences that students distinguish between **infinitives (Inf)** and **prepositional phrases (PP)** now or at any point in this course. However, if a teacher wants to make this distinction, it is important not to do so until the students have learned about **root (or base form) verbs (RV)** and **root verbals (RVbl)** in Chapter 4.

However, what is important, even imperative, is that students keep as many words in intact structures as possible and see meaningful chunks. This is especially important for their later being able to see **clauses** and **sentences.** What is important is their seeing intact structures, not their learning abstract rules, especially abstract rules beyond their **ceiling level.** Distinguishing between **prepositional phrases (PP)** and **infinitives (Inf),** especially at this time, serves no writing-centered purpose.

This is also true about distinguishing between **prepositional phrases (PP)** and d**ependent clauses (DC)** at this time. Until students have a firm understanding of the **phrase** structure and have learned about **subjects (S)** and **verbs (V)** (Chapters 3–5), they do not have the knowledge needed to identify **dependent clauses (DC).** However, after they acquire these foundational concepts, students can easily see the difference between **phrases** and **clauses** when they get to Chapter 7, which introduces **clauses.**

Thus, at this time it is premature and counterproductive to expect students to be able to distinguish between **dependent clauses (DC)** and **prepositional phrases (PP).** After all, except for the presence of a **subject-verb pair** and possibly a **complement** or **object** (Chapter 6), **dependent clauses (DC)** are made and identified by almost the same tools as **prepositional phrases (PP).** In fact, some subordinate conjunctions (called **dependent words (DW)** in this book) can even be **prepositions (P),** for example, "after" and "until." By the time students get to Chapter 7 they will have a clear concept of **subject-verb pairs, objects,** and **complements.** Students then can readily distinguish between the two structures.

Classwork 2-2, page 25

From now on, the **whole class** debriefing can include students' being invited to come up and write their own work on the board. It is important to say that if the volunteer makes a mistake it will be good because then people can learn something, reminding students of the **Natural Human Learning Process:** people learn through practice, through making and correcting mistakes.

It helps both the volunteer and the class when volunteers explain their analysis to the class. The teacher's then asking the class whether the analysis is correct according to the tools not only invites students to work together as a community but also keeps them actively involved and exercising their **critical thinking** skills.

In case no volunteers will come forward, the teacher might prepare by collecting interesting examples from students as he or she circulates during the **small group** work. A few good examples can always be found. Otherwise, as before, the teacher can ask students what they came up with and do the writing on the board as the students dictate. Also, as before, the students' work on the board can be used as examples for the tools being worked on.

After the **whole class** debriefing at the end of the activity, **Tools 10** and **11** can be introduced.

Tool 10: A connector (C) joins two or more of the same kind of thing that come before and after the connector (C): "and" and "or" are always connectors (C); "but" and "," are sometimes connectors (C).

Note: Students will see **compounds** more clearly if they number the things that are connected. They need to be careful to number them *only* when there is a **connector (C)** between the things.

Along with the examples for students to copy and **analyze I-SG-WC,** it is imperative for the students to practice considering the **connector (C)** question: "What are the two same things connected by the connector?"

Students, especially visual learners, will find a visual aid helpful (^—^—^). This **scaffolding** helps them construct their new **neural network** for the concept of **connectors (C).** Later, this scaffolding can be eliminated.

```
         P1  C   P2    —OP1—    C  —OP2—
The ball flew (up and over the house and the tree).
              ^__^___^        ^_____^____^
```

Students also might need a lot of help with the numbering of the two same things being connected **(Tool 10).** What seems to help is an emphasis on their numbering things *only* when there is a **connector (C)** between them. Conversely, they are never to number any things *unless* they have a **connector (C)** between them. This might seem like overkill, but students without concepts/**dendrites** for **compounds** need this guidance and support.

After the **whole class** debriefing of sufficient student examples, the students will have begun to gain a familiarity with **connectors (C).** First gaining a foundational understanding of **connectors (C)** helps students more easily understand the more complex structure of **compounds**. **Tool 11** can now be introduced.

Tool 11: Two same items connected by a connector (C) are called a "compound," such as compound preposition (cP), compound object of the preposition (cOP), and compound prepositional phrase (cPP).

To grow their **neural networks** and increase their fluency, students need to practice **analyzing** many **compounds;** for example, "She went in and out of the library very quickly" **(compound preposition [cP]).** "She went to the library and the bookstore" **(compound object of the preposition [cOP]).** "She went to the library and to the bookstore" **(compound prepositional phrase [cPP]).** "People travel with or without luggage or backpacks" **(compound preposition [cP] and compound object of the preposition [cOP]).**

It helps students develop their skill at using **Tool 11** if each example is given along with the **connector (C)** question: "What are the two same things connected by the connector? Those two same things are the compound." The students will need to use with precision the **compound** and **connector (C)** codes as they begin to construct their new **neural networks**.

$$(\text{————————PP————})$$
$$\text{————cP————}$$
$$\text{P1 C —P2— ——OP——}$$

She went (in and out of the library) very quickly.
$$\wedge—\wedge\text{————}\wedge$$

Students need to be reminded that an idea can be expressed in different ways, that writing is making choices.

$$(\text{————PP————————})$$
$$\text{——————————cOP————}$$
$$\text{P ——OP1— C ——OP2——}$$

She went (to the library and the bookstore).
$$\wedge\text{————}\wedge\text{————}\wedge$$

$$\text{————————cPP————————}$$
$$(\text{——PP1——}) \qquad (\text{——PP2——})$$
$$\text{P ——OP— C P ———OP——}$$

She went (to the library) and (to the bookstore).
$$\wedge\text{————}\wedge\text{————}\wedge$$

Some students have problems with the analysis, getting confused at first by all the coding **(C, cP, cOP, cPP).** However, it is imperative that students recognize **compounds** and the **connectors (C)** that create them. By working with **compounds** and **connectors (C)** from the beginning, students are constructing a foundation of skill and concepts that will later make it easy for them to recognize **compound subjects (CS)** and **compound verbs.** Thus, by the time they get to **sentences** in Chapter 7 they will have the skill and knowledge needed to easily recognize **compound sentences.**

A way that has proved helpful is to rationalize the coding in this way: The **c** in the code **(cP, cOP, cPP)** says there *must be* a **connector (C)** in order to have a **compound.** The rest of the code tells which part is the **compound.** Diagrams like these on the board can help make it clear:

```
  —cP—           ——cOP—         ——cPP—
  | \             | \            | \
 P1 C P2        OP1 C OP2      PP1 C PP2
```

More examples for students to copy in their book and to **analyze I-SG-WC** will help them construct their new **neural networks** for **compound** structures, for example,

```
     (———————————PP———————————)
       ———cP———     ———cOP———
        P1  C  P2    OP1   C  OP2
```
People travel (with or without luggage or backpacks).

```
        ——————PP—————
        ——————cOP—————
     P —OP1— C OP2 —C— OP3
```
She has lived (in New York, Iowa, and Michigan).

These codes are mnemonic devices to remind students that 1) whenever they see **connectors (C)** ("and" and "or" and sometimes "but" and ",") there is a **compound** and 2) there cannot be a **compound** unless there is a **connector (C).**

Classwork 2-2, page 25

These activities provide more practice to help students develop fluency, confidence, and a strong conceptual foundation for recognizing and writing **compounds.**

After the **whole class** debriefing at the end of Classwork 2-2 on page 27, **Tool 12** can be introduced.

Tool 12: Two or more same items in a compound are always in a list. Every item in a compound list must make sense when it is read alone with the rest of the sentence. Make sure you know where the compound list starts.

Students will need problems to solve for practice; for example, "I ate with Susanna, Diana, and Georgia. We went to Walt and Jessica's house."

```
     (———————PP———————)
        ———————cOP———————
     P  OP1   C OP2 —C— OP3
```
I ate (with Susanna, Diana, and   Georgia).   I ate with Susanna.   Yes
         ^___^___^__ ^_____^   I ate with Diana.   Yes
                                                   I ate with Georgia.   Yes
       start of ↑ list   This is a compound OP list.

$$(\text{———PP————})$$
$$\text{P ——OP—————}$$

We went (to Walt and Jessica's house).

We went to Walt.   No
We went to Jessica's house.
NOT only her house.   IT IS HIS, TOO.
This is not a **compound OP** list of two
OP's. It is one **OP**: "Walt and Jessica's
house" is one place.

Classwork 2-2, page 30

This might be a homework assignment or an in-class writing test.
Small group and **whole class** discussions are helpful even after a test.

Classwork 2-2, pages 32 and 33

Explaining their analysis is a **critical thinking** and **metacognitive**
activity that students say is very helpful. Explaining their analyses
helps students more firmly develop their concepts and skills.

Classwork 2-2, page 34

This activity makes a connection with the next chapter. Students need
to be reminded that there are different correct ways to **analyze** this
sentence and that each student should use his or her own sense of logic.

———PP———   —PP—   —PP—   ———PP—— —PP—
(After working) (at home) (with Li), he ran (for a mile) (for exercise).

or

————————PP————————   ————————PP————————
(After working at home with Li), he ran (for a mile for exercise).

After the **whole class** debriefing, the teacher can explain that what
is left is what makes this sentence grammatically correct ("he ran"): a
subject (S) and a **verb (V)**. The teacher can explain that **prepositional phrases (PP)** add interesting and important information to a
sentence but that they do not make the sentence grammatically correct. The teacher might want to inform the students that in the next
chapters they will learn about the most important parts of a sentence:
subjects (S) and **verbs (V).**

Finally, it is important for students to begin thinking of the parentheses around **prepositional phrases (PP)** as iron bars or cages
around them. This idea will be important later when students study
subjects (S) and **verbs (V).** This is the substance of **Tool 19** in
Chapter 3; it is a very important and helpful tool that keeps students
from making serious errors misidentifying **objects of the preposition (OP)** as **subjects (S)** or **verbs (V).**

Prepositional Phrase Comments

Over the years a number of teachers who were using earlier drafts of
this book called or wrote me with questions. This section contains all
my responses to their questions. Perhaps these will be of use to you.

After learning about the six stages of the **Natural Human Learning Process,** students readily accept that they need to start at the lowest stage in learning anything new.

Students need to know that there are **conventions** (called "rules") made up by people—but that sentences *must* follow them. They need to know that the conventions are iron and can't be broken. They also need to know that they will use them correctly if they follow the tools they learn in this course. These tools will save them (grammatically speaking)!

The goal of this first unit is to learn to **analyze** (identify)—and put parentheses around—every **prepositional phrase (PP)** in the students' own writing. To do this they need to identify the tools (characteristics or elements of the **PP schema**). These tools need to be repeated and referred to continually. Students must become totally familiar and comfortable with these tools for identifying a **PP**. Repeated trial-and-error practice with feedback is needed to construct the **schema** and its underlying **neural network**.

Idioms need to be discussed when they arise: "Every language has special ways of saying things that can't be explained by tools. You just have to memorize them. For example, Americans say, `Don't pull my leg.' What does that mean?" Someone will probably know. Remind students that there is a place at the back of the book where they can record the **idioms** they want to remember, for example, "in the evening," "at night," "care for you," "care about you," "talk about it," "discuss it."

Special cases: "I will wake (up the kids) "instead of "wake up" as an **idiomatic verb (V)**. This treatment of such **verbs (V)**, using the **prepositional phrase (PP)** tools they are learning, seems less confusing, especially at this point in students' learning when their **ceiling level** is low.

At the start of each class, put on the board a list of new **prepositions (P)** and "**never-prepositions**" (words or categories) from errors in students' homework, e.g., "a," "an," and "the"; all words ending in "ing" except "concerning," "considering," "during," "regarding," "relating to"; all action words; all person, place, and thing words; "more," "most," "and," "also," "but," "next," "which," "who." Students should copy these into the list of "**never-prepositions.**" Students must study and use the lists so they can recognize **prepositions (P)** and "**never-prepositions.**"

As important as is the list of **prepositions (P)**, an equally important list is the list of "**never-prepositions.**" Unfortunately, the "**never-prepositions**" list is as long as the dictionary minus **prepositions (P)**!

When many of our basic students start this chapter, they have no concept of, and no **neural networks** for, **PP's**—nor any other sentence structure or element. We need to take them from that point to the point of their being able to identify **PP's** when they see them in their own writing. While we are trying to lead them, via their trial-and-error-with-feedback exploration, toward the construction of this new **neural network** and **schema**, we need to keep pushing the "**never prepositions**" out of their way so they can see the **prepositions (P)** more clearly.

Typically students misidentify **articles, adjectives (Adj),** and **adverbs (Adv)** as **prepositions (P)**. But it does no good to try to have students distinguish between these elements—because that would be totally confusing and totally unsuccessful at this point. In fact, there is usually little or no time in this course to address **adjectives (Adj)** and **adverbs (Adv)**. The students, though, will be able to learn them easily enough in later courses after they acquire the firm foundation of basic concepts in this course. (Classwork 9-2 in Chapter 9 introduces **adjectives [Adj]** and **adverbs [Adv]** as an optional section.)

What the students need to do is become familiar with both **prepositions (P)** and "**never prepositions**" that arise in their writing.

The earliest **small group** activities might take only one minute. But it is essential that students always follow this three-step sequence: **individual** work, **small group** sharing and helping, **whole class** debriefing and discussion with questions and answers.

One tool says that a word can be a **preposition (P)** only if there is an **object of the preposition (OP)**. We know this isn't necessarily true, that in a student sentence like "She looked at the room which she found herself in" the "in" *is* a **preposition (P)**. But by our tool it *cannot* be because if you ask "what or whom?" after the **preposition (P)** there is nothing there; no **object of the preposition (OP)** follows it, which another tool says it *must* (the **object of the preposition [OP]** must end the **prepositional phrase [PP]**).

"She looked at the room which she found herself in": Do you have to bite your tongue to tell the students that "in" is *not* a **preposition (P)** in this sentence (by the tool that a **P** must be followed by its **OP**)? Do you have to bite your tongue so you don't say, "But the understood object of the preposition is 'which' in the recast, and formally correct, sentence, 'She looked at the room in which she found herself'"?

Yes! At this point in students' development you do! Remember, the premise of this approach is that students are acquiring new brain structures and conceptual **schemas**. They are building a solid new basis for firm footing through the grammatical-sentence swamp, one small spot at a time. Any straying from this single-minded task and purpose leads them into only confusion. But after they have got their footing and enough clear and solid ground to have confidence and balance, then the fine-tuning and the more intricate details can easily be added. At that point they will have such a rich **schema** or **neural network** that they will say, "Oh, I see. Sure. No problem" to points that at the beginning of their **schema**-construction they would respond to by saying, "I don't know what you're talking about! I'm lost and overwhelmed!"

I say, "In this class, words are called **prepositions** (or whatever element or structure we are working on) only if they follow our tools. Learning grammar this way will help you learn to write correctly even if it isn't the way grammar is usually taught."

Students with good rote or theoretical grammar knowledge might look askance at you. It will help if you make these points to the class: "Some of you have excellent grammar knowledge, but your writing isn't showing it yet or doesn't read like good English writing yet. And some of you might write pretty well but don't have good grammar knowledge. There's a wide range in this class—and only a short time. This method will help you grow the dendrites you need to express yourselves in correct sentences in the time that we have. This method really works. Just hang in there, and you will see how well it works as we go on."

In this class, I've had students who have taken one or two quarters of freshman composition but who say they feel like a sham because they have little or no conscious knowledge of grammar. I warn them they might be bored by this class, but they assure me they won't be. And they aren't. This curriculum is very challenging and exciting— especially as students feel themselves learning and can see their understanding grow from day to day. Also, the delivery method is full of activity for the students.

At this point, students will be identifying **dependent clauses (DC)** and **infinitives (Inf)** as **PP's** because the same tools apply. And this is perfectly fine, exactly right! They are correctly applying their tools. This is the critical activity they must learn to do—applying tools with absolute clarity and precision. Later on, after they have acquired some solid ground to stand on, it becomes easy for them, with a few more tools, to distinguish between **dependent clauses (DC), infinitives (Inf),** and **PP's.**

There are some **tricky words** (to be identified as such) that must be introduced separately with special attention: "like," "that," "so," etc. These **tricky words** are on a separate **tricky words** list in the "Toolbook."

The explanation to help students with these words, and with their **analyses** in general, is the following, to be reinforced and repeated throughout the course: "You can't know what a word is until you see what it is doing in the sentence. And you know what it is doing in the sentence by knowing and applying the tools" **(Tool 4).**

It will do no good at this point to give explanations that include discussion of **verbs (V), relative pronouns, adjectives (Adj),** and **subordinating conjunctions.** Either the students won't understand these words because they have no **schemas** or **neural networks** for them and will experience only the frustration of cognitive drowning, or ESL students will use only their rote or theoretical knowledge.

The students must continually be reminded that 1) this class is to learn just what is needed for them to be able to write correct sentences and 2) if they want to know more about grammar as an abstract subject rather than to learn how to use it for writing correctly, then they need to take a grammar-for-grammar course instead of, or after, this writing course.

Each day I start class by returning the previous day's corrected homework and putting samples from that homework on the board for the class to "solve," i.e., **analyze**. Students prefer boardwork to be correct sentences rather than incorrect sentences, which they say confuse them. However, when students go to the board to **analyze** and happen to make errors, others in the class should correct them. "What a good mistake," I say. "This helps us learn. Thank you for the good mistake!"

At this point in the course, the "sentences" they write are whatever they think a sentence is. Only later do we work on what sentences really are.

The most difficult students to teach with this method are ESL students who are better in rote or theoretical grammar than in writing fluently and correctly. They feel confident and have high self-esteem when discussing grammar theoretically and in the abstract but feel unconfident and inexpert when asked to express themselves fluently in correct grammar, which is the goal of this curriculum. This curriculum attempts to ignore their highly developed abstract knowledge and, instead, tries to help them construct a new grammar skill that is writing-based. This curriculum asks them to put aside all they can do well and do something strange and difficult. Their abstract knowledge can be counterproductive.

These students, quite understandably, resist this approach. They present a problem for the class because they want to bring the subject to their strength: they want to have high-level grammar discussions; they want theoretical explanations. This is a problem for the teacher, who might not be prepared for such discussions and might feel at a loss. It is a problem for the other students because they do not know what is going on and feel the distress of cognitive drowning. It is a problem for the curriculum because it distracts attention from skill development and uses up precious time on something that is essentially irrelevant to the work and goal at hand.

The teacher needs to keep the students focused on the work and goal at hand. The teacher will need to keep reminding students about the difference between abstract knowledge and writing skill knowledge, about having to grow **dendrites** from the bottom up, about having to make mistakes, start simply, practice, and practice. When students persist in asking questions outside the scope of the curriculum, an appropriate response is to remind them that this is a grammar-for-writing course and not a pure grammar course. Discussing their feelings with them in your office is also very helpful.

The signing deaf don't use English syntax; they are like ESL students because American Sign Language does not use English syntax.

Whenever students make a mistake **analyzing** (identifying) their **PP's,** it will be because they aren't following the tools. For example, they might need to be reminded that a **preposition (P)** must be the first word of the **PP**, that the **OP** must be the entire answer to "what or whom?" after the **preposition (P)**, that the **preposition (P)** will be found on the **preposition (P)** list. (They might come up with a **preposition (P)** that is not on the list. If so, add it and let me know!)

At this point in their skill development students are becoming able to conceptualize and recognize chunks (grammatical elements and structures). "This is a consummation devoutly to be wished."

We can't overestimate their lack of knowledge and potential confusion and how easily they can get off the track. A great deal of activity is going on inside their brain as new neural structures are trying to form.

When using the abbreviations **PP's** or **P's** or **OP's**, explain that the way to make a **plural** of a nonword (like these letters) is to add "'s."

Some students will want to say that a row of **PP's** can be the whole **OP** for one **P:** "(in the room down the hall on the first floor)." Or they might **analyze** it as small **PP's** inside bigger ones: "(in the room (down the hall) (on the first floor))" or "(in the room (down the hall (on the first floor)))." Or they might **analyze** each one separately. I tell students they don't have to put small **PP's** inside big ones—they can leave all the **PP's** as small ones. Different ways are correct. So why bring it up? Because students' sense of logic must be supported. Every student must feel confident about relying on his/her sense of logic.

$$(\quad P \quad \text{—}OP\text{—}) (P \text{———} OP\text{—}) (P \quad OP)$$
The man is (under the log) (on the ground) (near him).

$$(\quad P \quad \text{————} OP\text{————————}) $$
The man is (under the log (on the ground (near him))).

I call the initial **preposition (P)** the "granddaddy preposition," and students know what that means—and laugh. But they must always be careful about having the **object of preposition (OP)** answer "what or whom?" after the **preposition (P)**.

Students will have problems with **compounds:** they will at first not see it at all; then, as they practice, they will begin to see it; they will want you to clarify that the **C (connector)** is between PP's. "Yes, the connector is between two PP's." They will want you to clarify that the **C** is between **OP's** inside one **PP**. "Yes, the connector can also be inside one PP, between two OP's—and also between two P's." After they have practiced awhile, ask them where they are on the **ceiling-level** diagram and where they were when they started **PP's**. They will be beginning to feel they're learning it.

You must warn students that **connectors (C)** can join things other than **prepositions (P), objects of prepositions (OP),** and **prepositional phrases (PP),** so students must be careful—they will learn the other things later.

Clarify and reinforce the understanding that the parentheses around **prepositional phrases (PP)** are like iron cages—anything inside them stays locked together inside and can't get out of them.

No word inside a PP can be used with a word outside its **PP**. Words inside a **PP** can work only with other words inside the same **PP (Tool 15** in Chapter 3).

Here is what planning for a class looks like. It lists what I plan to do the next day, sentences to put on the board, new tools, new words for lists. I make these plans while I am correcting my students' homework before the next class.

1. "Never-prepositions" on the board to add to students' "never-prepositions" list:
   often
   but (They are going, but Mary is staying home. "But" is a **P** *only* if it means "except for"—They are all going but Mary.)
   words that end in "ly"
   for (not if it means "because": I will do it for you asked me to. "For" is a **P** *only* if it *doesn't* mean "because": I will do it for you.)
   words for people, and things, e.g., I, it, he, she, Joe, the pets

2. Always check your **P's** with the **preposition (P)** and "**never-preposition**" lists!

3. Your mistakes bring you closer to correct understanding as you correct and learn from them.

4. Tool: A **preposition (P)** never has "a," "an," or "the" in front of it.
(I often make up a new tool if I see students need one! The *only* explanation should be a tool.)

5. On the board for **I-SG-WG:**

Outside it is raining. Tell students to ask "what?" after **P**. If no answer, there is no **P**. Just because a word is on the list doesn't mean it *has* to be a **P**. It's a **P** *only* if there is an answer to "what?" or "whom?" after it.

6. Students write their own sentence using "outside" as **P: I-SG-WC**

$$(P \quad OP) \quad \textbf{No!}$$

7. I cleaned my room up yesterday. ("yesterday" doesn't answer "what?")

$$(P \ OP) \qquad \textbf{Yes}$$

I cleaned up my room yesterday. ("my room" answers "what?")

Tell students: You can write any sentence in different ways. But tools go with the exact words you have actually written down.

$$\overline{}P\overline{} \ \overline{}OP1\overline{} \ C \ OP2$$

8. (Next to the field and yard) were the barn and house.

$$P \ \overline{}OP1\overline{} \quad C \ OP2$$

Men and women are (inside the stores and cars).

$$\begin{array}{ccc} PP1 & & PP2 \\ P \ \overline{}OP\overline{} & C & P \quad OP \end{array}$$

I ran (to the store) and (back home). (Add "back" to **preposition (P)** list when it's used like this.)

$$P1 \ C \ P2 \ \overline{}OP\overline{}$$

She went (in and out the door).

$$P1 \ C \ P2 \quad \overline{}OP1\overline{} \quad C \ OP2$$

They climbed (up and down the stairs and ladders).

$$P \ \overline{}OP\overline{}$$

9. I went (to the game) and ate hot dogs.   (to what? "the game" = end of **PP**)

They studied (at the library) and did well (on the test). (end of **PP** with answer to "what?": at what? the "library" = end of **PP**)

10. $(P \overline{} OP \overline{})$ (**OP** is whole answer to

$$P \ OP \qquad \text{"what/whom?" asked}$$

He gave it (to someone who knows how (to do it)).   after the **P**.)

Stopping to answer students' questions is essential. In fact, their questions can *be* the lesson! However, questions about elements beyond their ceiling level should be postponed until those elements are introduced in the textbook.

SUBJECTS AND VERBS 1

Chapter 3 focuses on helping students begin to construct a foundation for understanding and correctly using **subjects (S)** and **verbs (V)**. One major goal of Chapter 3 is to help students recognize and correctly use different verb forms, including **verbals (Vbl)**. This chapter introduces the **"be" helper (BH)**, the **present participle** (here called the **continuing verb [CV])**, and the **verbal (Vbl)** derived from the **present participle** (here called the **continuing verbal [CVbl])**. Using logical and **tense**-neutral terms (for example, "continuing" instead of "present" or "progressive") is helpful. For example, students have difficulty understanding the logic of why "I was going" is **past tense** but uses the **present participle**.

Chapter 3 introduces **number** and **tense** but not **person**, and it does not go into great depth about **tense.** The rationale for this approach is that these are the necessary foundational concepts for very complex sentence elements and that it would be premature and counterproductive to introduce these complex elements now. However, with this foundation in place, students can later more easily learn the more complex particularities of **tense** in Chapter 11. (Classwork 11-1 and 11-2 in Chapter 11 are optional resources that an instructor might want to include with Chapter 3.)

Full debriefing by students of their work and full exploration of their questions in relation to the tools are essential for their learning to understand and use the tools. Also, students find it helpful when each class begins with a few sentences from their previous homework on the board or overhead for them to solve **individually**, in **small groups**, and then as a **whole class**. The teacher can always find in their homework certain sentences that will provide good examples to illustrate the correct use of the tools. If necessary, the teacher can revise these sentences somewhat to make them better examples.

The learning activities in this chapter, as in all subsequent chapters, follow the pattern, described in detail in Chapter 2, of sequences of **individual, small group,** and **whole class (I-SG-WC)**.

Note: During the **small group** work teachers find that as soon as they have worked with a group which has asked for help, the group will want to get back to working on the problem by themselves. As the theory and research show, learners who are active and interactive learn well.

Classwork 3-1, page 49

For the **whole class** activity the teacher might write two to three student sentences on the board, for example, "The woman is running."

Then, after the **whole class** debriefing, **Tools 13** and **14** can be introduced.

Tool 13: To find the subject (S) and the verb (V), ask, "Who or what is, was, or will be doing something?" The whole answer to "who?" or "what?" is the subject (S).

The class might now be invited to identify the **subject (S)** in each sentence just written on the board, one sentence at a time, with discussion and questions, if they have any, after each one; for example,

S

The <u>woman</u> is running.

It might be pointed out that, while "woman" is the main part of the **subject (S),** students should include all the words that go together as the **subject (S)** to keep together as many words as possible. This will let them use their logic and also help them see structures or chunks of meaning in a sentence rather than just single, isolated words. Being able to see words in chunks or structures is a more critical—and practical—skill for writing than is being able to identify isolated grammatical elements.

Students will now be ready to try to identify the **subject (S)** in their own sentence that they wrote in their book (**S** over the **whole subject** and one line under it). They can then check with neighbors and, finally, ask any questions they might have in the **whole class** debriefing.

Students will now be ready for **Tool 14.**

Tool 14: What the subject (S) is doing is the verb (V).

The class might be invited to identify the **verbs (V)** in the sentences on the board, one by one as before, making no distinction at this point between simple **verbs (V)** and **helper-participle** combination **verbs (V).**

The visual aid beneath the sentence shows which **subject (S)** and **verb (V)** go together. This helps students, especially the visually oriented, construct their **neural networks** for **subject-verb pairs.** Recognizing **subject-verb pairs** is the foundational concept for later recognizing **clauses** and, thus, sentences.

——S—— ——V——
The <u>woman</u> <u>is running</u>.
^————————^

Then students will be ready to identify the **verb (V)** in their own sentence that they wrote in their book (**V** over the **whole verb** and two lines under it). Have students check with neighbors and then ask any questions they might have during the **whole class** debriefing.

A **"Never-a-Verb List"** is invaluable. Such a list appears on page 78 followed by a space for students to list any other **"never-verbs"** that are confusing to them.

Tool 15: A subject (S) and its verb V must both be inside or both outside the same PP. No word inside a PP can be used with a word outside its PP. Words inside a PP can work only with words inside the same PP: (S) V No; S (V) No; (SV) Yes; (SV) Yes

Students find **Tool 15** very helpful because mistakes related to this tool often come up along the way and can be corrected easily with this simple, clear point: both **subject (S)** and **verb (V)** must be either both inside the same **prepositional phrase (PP)** or both outside the **prepositional phrase (PP)**. If the **subject (S)** and the **verb (V)** are inside a **prepositional phrase (PP)**, it is not a **phrase**, of course, but a **clause**. But until students have become secure in their ability to recognize **subjects (S)** and **verbs (V)**, making this distinction is premature and counterproductive. When they reach Chapter 7, however, they will readily be able to see the difference between **phrases** and **clauses**. In this way, students have the opportunity to construct foundational concepts about the structures or chunks of meaning in a sentence. On this foundation students can later add more complex, refined concepts and terminology. The only harm done now is to the teacher, who has to bite his or her tongue when introducing this strange—but extremely helpful—tool.

Classwork 3-1, page 51

For the **individual** activity students can **analyze** for both **subject (S)** and **verb (V)**. If some students see the **subject (S)** as a **compound**, they might find **analyzing** it challenging because they haven't yet **analyzed** a **compound subject (cS)**. But a challenge slightly above their **ceiling level**—and any resulting mistakes—will stimulate their **dendrites** to start growing and connecting for this new knowledge. The **small group** work will give them the opportunity to do interactive processing, which stimulates learning.

For the **whole class** activity, volunteers might be asked to write their sentence and **analysis** on the board. Then the class might be asked to comment and ask questions, as always referring to and using their tools.

If no student has a **compound subject (cS)**, and if the teacher wants to use the explore/experiment approach, it will be necessary for the teacher to write one or two sentences on the board to be **analyzed I-SG-WC**; for example, "Paul and Yang are singing." Students might be reminded to review and use the **compound** tool from Chapter 2.

```
               ———cS———
           S1    C   S2  ——V——
          Paul and Yang are singing.
               ^_____^
```

More samples might now be provided for their **dendrite**-growing practice; for example, "Jo and I sang and danced in the show." "You and Ty study and work a lot."

```
—cS—        ——cV——        ——cS——       —cV————
S1  C  S2  V1   C   V2   ——PP—   S1  C  S2  V1   C   V2
Jo and I sang and danced (in the show).  "You and Ty study and work a lot."
   ^_____^                             ^_____^
```

> **Note:** If students misspell "a lot," they will appreciate the mnemonic device that "a lot" (commonly misspelled as "alot") is "a lot of words."

Classwork 3-1, page 49

Sentences like these reinforce the important tool that what a word is depends on how it is used in a sentence. **Tool 15** is very helpful; the **subject (S)** and its **verb (V)** must both be together inside a **prepositional phrase (PP)** or both be outside it. Students are entertained by and learn from the following sentences.

```
——S—— V  ——PP——            ——S—— V
The arrow flies (like the wind).   The fruit flies like a banana.
    ^_____^                          ^_____^
```

```
       S V     (P  —OP—)
       I like you (like a friend).
       ^—^
```

> **Note:** "Like" is a **tricky word**. Students might be directed to look at the list of **tricky words** in the "Toolbook."

Classwork 3-2, page 54

Students will benefit from periodic reminders that careful practice is absolutely essential for learning.

After the **whole class** debriefing at the end of Classwork 3-2, students are ready for **Tools 16** and **17**.

> **Tool 16: A verb (V) that ends in "ing" must have a "be" verb with it as its "helper verb." A verb (V) that ends in "ing" is called a "continuing verb" (CV). "Continuing" means the verb (V) is continuing over a period of time. The "be" helper verb (BH) and its continuing verb (CV) go together to make the whole verb: BH + CV = V.**

> **Note:** There are nine "be" verbs.

The students will need the list of **"be" helper verbs (BH),** which the teacher might write on the board or have on an overhead for students to copy in their book. Students can be informed that this list is in **Tool 16** in the "Toolbook."

Note: "Get" and "keep" are listed in **Tool 16** in the "Toolbook" as **verbs (V)** that act like **"be" verbs**: She keeps going. Let's get going.

"Be" Helper Verbs

am, are, is, was, were, will be, been, being
("being" helps a different **verb (V)**; more on this later)

Students will now be ready to **analyze I-SG-WC** the sentences on the board for **"be" helpers (BH)** and **continuing verbs (CV)**.

Tool 17: Every "be" verb is always a verb (V). A "be" verb is either a verb (V) by itself or a "be" helper verb (BH). There are three exceptions: "be," "been," "being." These are never verbs (V) by themselves; they are only helper verbs (HV).

Note: In case the question arises, the teacher can point out that **"be" verbs** do not answer the question, "Who or what is doing something?" (In an order, "be" can be seen as a verb [V]: "Be there!")

Tool 18, addressing **number agreement**, is one of the most important tools. Students should now focus in each sentence on **number agreement**.

Tool 18: Every subject (S) has number: it is either singular (s— only one) or plural (p—than one). The verb (V) or helper verb (HV) must have the same number as its subject (S). This is called "number agreement."

Note: Students will need to study and use this first note to this tool: Almost every **singular (s) verb (V)** in the **present tense** ends in "s" except when the **subject (S)** is "I" or "you." **"Present tense"** means the **subject (S)** does the **verb (V)** usually or generally.

Students will benefit from examples to **analyze I-SG-WC;** for example,

$$\overset{s}{\underline{\text{Sara}}} \; \overset{s}{\underline{\text{wants}}} \text{ attention.} \qquad \overset{\overline{\hspace{1em}p\hspace{1em}}}{\underline{\text{Lubova and Sergei}}} \; \overset{p}{\underline{\text{want}}} \text{ a vacation.}$$

$$\overset{s}{\underline{\text{I}}} \; \overset{s}{\underline{\text{need}}} \text{ time.} \qquad \overset{s}{\underline{\text{You}}} \; \overset{s}{\underline{\text{need}}} \text{ a good education.}$$

Note: Again, it would be premature and counterproductive to introduce complex and refined work on **number, tense,** and **person** at this point. After students have constructed firm foundational concepts in these early chapters, they will be well able to construct higher-level concepts in Chapter 11,which focuses on **tense** and **person**.

However, if the teacher wants at this point to do more work on **person, person agreement,** or **tense** he or she might want to interpose Classwork 11-1 in Chapter 11.

Classwork 3-3, page 61

After the **whole class** debriefing, **Tools 19** and **20** can be introduced.

Tool 19: There can be only one subject (S) for each verb (V) and only one verb (V) for each subject (S)—unless there is a compound subject (cS) or a compound verb (cV).

Tool 20: Put a connector (C) between subject-verb pairs just as between any other compounds. Put a comma before the connector (C) between subject-verb pairs. (Use the compound tools introduced in Chapter 2.)

The teacher might provide students with other examples to **analyze I-SG-WC**. As in the following example, students are looking only for elements and structures they have learned about so far. To ask them to look for **compound sentences** at this time would be premature and counterproductive. However, students are constructing **neural networks** for **compounds** and, later, when they get to Chapter 7, they will readily have the ability to see **compound sentences**.

$$\overline{}\text{Compound Subject-Verb (cSV)}\overline{}$$
$$\overline{}\text{SV1}\overline{}\qquad\qquad \text{C}\ \ \overline{}\text{SV1}\overline{}$$

Ron read my paper, and Pam read Jim's paper.

Note: As with **prepositional compounds,** the teacher can expect that students will need to be reminded that if there is no **connector (C)**, there is no **compound** and so there is no **numbering.**

Classwork 3-3, page 61

After the **whole class** debriefing, in order to prepare students, ultimately, to be able to recognize **compound sentences,** they will need more practice with **compounds** of all kinds—**compound subjects (cS), compound verbs (cV), compound continuing verbs (cCV).** This will increase students' fluency, control, and confidence. The teacher might write more problems on the board for students to solve **I-SG-WC.**

Also, at this point students who are **analyzing** correctly can omit the scaffolding of the visual aid beneath the sentence. They might also omit the **number** scaffolding except for **present tense verbs.** Unless the teacher prefers otherwise, students can omit the scaffolding for **tense.**

$$\overline{}\text{cS}\overline{}\qquad\qquad \overline{}\text{cCV}\overline{}$$
$$\text{S1}\ \ \text{C}\ \ \text{S2}-\text{BH}-\qquad\text{CV1}\qquad\text{C}\qquad\text{CV2}\qquad\qquad\qquad\overline{}\text{cOP}\overline{}$$

You and I will be studying and talking together (with Jon and Mai).

$$\overline{}\text{cSV}\overline{}$$
$$\overline{}\text{SV1}\overline{}\qquad\qquad\overline{}\text{SV2}\overline{}$$
$$\overline{}\text{cCV}\overline{}$$
$$\text{BH}\quad\text{CV1}\quad\text{C}\quad\text{CV2}\qquad\qquad\text{C}\ \ \text{S}\ \ \text{V}$$

They were reading and writing all night, and it was fun.

This analysis might seem excessively complicated. But students enjoy the challenge, especially when they feel themselves becoming more and more able to know what they are doing. The talking they do in their **small groups** and as a **whole class**—as they check their notes and tools, think it through, puzzle over it, debate about it—is one of the most powerful learning activities they can do.

Classwork 3-4, page 66

After the **whole class** debriefing at the end of Classwork 3-4, **Tools 21** and **22** can be introduced.

Tool 21: Without a "be" verb on the left helping it, the "ing" verblike word is not a verb (V) in that sentence. It is a verbal (Vbl) instead. A verbal (Vbl) can be a subject (S) or an object of the preposition (OP).

The goal for this section, as in the analogous sections in Chapter 4 and 5, is for students to be able to distinguish between **verbs (V)** and **verbals (Vbl).** This is imperative because students' success at seeing **clauses** and **sentences** and, ultimately, avoiding **sentence-boundary errors,** depends on their being able to recognize **subject-verb** structures. Their chances for success are better if they are aware of, and not confused by, **verbals (Vbl).**

Note: Tool 21 in the "Toolbook" adds that a **verbal (Vbl)** that is a **subject (S)** or an **object of the preposition (OP)** is called a "gerund." The teacher might think it is important that students know that term. However, at this early stage in their learning, abstract, noncommonsensical terminology has a dampening effect on students.

   Because the book does not introduce **direct objects** (Chapter 6) and **adjectives (Adj)** (Chapter 9) until later, these terms are not used at this time.

Tool 22: A verb (V) can never be a description of the subject (S). A verb (V) tells what the subject (S) is doing or else it is a "be" verb.

Students will benefit from more problems to solve; for example,

—————S————— V   S BH   CV   ——PP——
The running water was cold. Last year I was always biking (to school).

S   V
We entered the biking race.

Subjects and Verbs Comments

Reiterate that what a word is can be known only by how it is used in a **sentence (Tool 4).**

   Nouns and **predicates** are theoretically interesting concepts, but students do not need to know what they are in order to write correctly. Because time is at a premium in this course and because the fundamental concepts and skills students need to acquire are so numerous, content that is mainly of theoretical interest seems dispensable. (**Nouns** are introduced in connection with **pronouns** in Chapter 6)

Students need continually to be reminded that if they don't know what a word is, they should leave it alone and not **analyze** it.

"Not" can be seen as part of the **verb (V)**. This is for students for whom "not" seems part of the action—to them it seems the anti-action or the action-in-negative. It makes sense to them. And one of the tenets of this approach is that students' common sense and logic must be supported as major resources for their successful learning. To students for whom "no" doesn't seem part of the **verb (V),** I say they don't have to call it a **verb (V)**. They simply don't **analyze** it. If, however, they feel it is part of the **verb (V)**, then they may call it that.

But I have to make it clear that this type of choice-making can't be used with most of the things students are learning. Most tools are "like iron." However, I keep reinforcing the idea that writing is making choices, that an idea can be expressed in many different ways. This point becomes even more clear when we get to **dependent clauses (DC)** and punctuation.

** Here's a typical mistake:

$$\begin{array}{ccc} S & HV & V \\ \text{Kieu} & \text{is} & \text{smart.} \end{array} \quad \begin{array}{ccc} S & HV & V \\ \text{I} & \text{am} & \text{tired.} \end{array}$$

How can we discuss this sticky mistake when the students don't know what **predicate nominatives** and **predicate adjectives** are? We do it easily by clarifying what **verbs (V)** are: "Is 'smart' (or 'tired') an action that the subject is doing, or is it a description of how the subject is?" Students' logic and common sense invariably provide the correct answer. Another way to help them see this is to use the tool that **"be" helper verbs (BH)** use a **continuing ("ing") verb (Tool 16).**

This sticky problem is complicated, especially for ESL students, when the students' common sense says a particular nonverb is, in fact, a **verb (V)**.

$$\begin{array}{ccc} S & BH & V \\ \text{It} & \text{was} & \text{fun today.} \end{array} \qquad \begin{array}{cccc} S & BH & HV & V \\ \text{We} & \text{were} & \text{having} & \text{fun.} \end{array}$$

"Fun" isn't an action word, but students' common sense tells them that "fun" is an action! And the **subject (S)** is doing it. A student's common sense must always be supported, even when not everyone agrees with him or her. So another way to make the distinction clear is to explain that there are specific tools for **verbs (V)** and that when students write they must use these tools, like a **continuing ("ing") verb** being the only kind of **verb (V)** after a **"be" helper verb (BH) (Tool 16)**. (When they study the **passive verb** in Chapter 5, **Tool 16** can easily be seen to have one exception.)

A useful technique for testing for a **verb (V)** is to put "I" in front of it and see whether it works for different times:

Yesterday I funned.   **No!**   (Usually the students will recognize
Today I fun.   **No!**   that this doesn't work. If an ESL stu
Tomorrow I will fun.   **No!**   dent can't see this, he or she perhaps
                                  needs a basic ESL course.)

vs.

Yesterday I had it.   Yesterday I worked.
Today I have it.   Today I work.
Tomorrow I will have it.   Tomorrow I will work.

Some **idioms** are exceptions to this test:
"supposed to," "used to"

S——V——   S ——V——
I am supposed (to do it).   They are supposed (to go).

S ——V——   S ——V——
He was used (to working). You will be used (to it).

In Chapter 5 students will also learn about **passives,** which do
not follow **Tool 16** that **BH's** help only "ing" (**continuing**)
verbs (CV).

Unfortunately, though, this test doesn't work for every word:

Yesterday I tired.   (Instead of "Yesterday I was tired." But it
                              could be correct, couldn't it? "Yesterday I
                              tired quickly.")
Today I tire.   (a **verb [V]**)
Tomorrow I will tire.   (a **verb [V]**).

However, if students intend to describe the **subject (S)** rather than
tell what the **subject (S)** is doing, then it cannot be a **verb (V)**. In
Chapter 6 they will learn about **complements**; it is counterproductive to explain or to name this concept prematurely.
　Verbals (Vbl) are very difficult, especially for ESL students. To
try to unravel and clarify this sentence element by referring to
gerunds would only lead to less time for the essentials because
although **gerunds** are theoretically interesting, they do not help students write with correct grammar.
　If a student cannot see that a particular **verbal (Vbl)** is not a **verb
(V)**, it might help to explain that if it follows the tool and makes
sense, call it a **verb (V)** for now. Later in the course when students
know more, it becomes easier for them to identify **verbals (Vbl)**.
The choice at this point is either to try to force students to accept,
without understanding, what the teacher says or to help them learn
to rely on their common sense.

The latter requires that we let them make and learn from their mistakes while they are bit-by-bit growing and connecting their new **dendrites** and **synapses** until they have enough to eventually see the picture more clearly.

Maybe an inexperienced student's common sense and logic shouldn't be relied upon. But if people can't rely on these, what can they rely on? A key factor in being an independent—and confident—thinker is being able to trust one's common sense and logic. As students' confidence increases, as their **dendrites** and **synapses** increase, as their common sense and logic have richer **neural networks** to inform them, they will see more and more clearly and correctly. It's a step-by-step process.

Students must also be able to rely on their common sense to give them the whole answer to "What is the **subject** of the **verb?**" (as well as to "what/whom?" after the **preposition [P]).** In later chapters they will learn to ask "what?" after other sentence elements. But, as always, it is critical for students to construct a firm foundation before branching out.

Sometimes students want to rewrite another student's sentences or a sentence on the board. I tell them that we could write this same idea—or any idea—in many different ways. But this sentence is this way, so that's what we have to deal with and **analyze** here. In fact, students will get opportunities later to see the many different ways they can write a sentence.

A related problem is that students will sometimes **analyze** what they understand the sentence to be saying, not what the actual words are. I remind them that the analyses must be based on the words that are actually written down.

Don't underestimate students' lack of knowledge and how much time and practice are needed to construct new brain structures. For example, when students do not know what **subjects (S)** and **verbs (V)** are (do not have **neural networks** and **schemas** for these concepts), they will need a lot of practice and processing to learn.

I tell my students that we are building up to the main tools in the class, which they will start to learn in a few weeks. To get ready for this, they need to get **prepositional phrases (PP)** and **subjects (S)** and **verbs (V)** firmly in mind first—and then the main tools will be learned fairly quickly and easily. Otherwise, the main tools will be very difficult to learn. The main tools are about **clauses** and the three **boundary errors: fragments, run-ons,** and **comma splices.** Identifying **sentence boundary errors** depends on understanding **clauses,** which depends on identifying **subjects (S)** and **verbs (V).**

Be sure not to have too many new things each day. Students need time to practice (do it themselves, talk about it, get feedback, try it again) and then to consolidate with even more practice. The **individual, small group,** and **whole class** activities in this *Instructor's Manual* provide the opportunities for this practice and consolidation.

Students need to be reminded always to ask: "What is this sentence about: Who/what is doing/being what?"

Here is a sequence for finding **subjects (S)** and **verbs (V)**:

1. Find the **prepositional phrases (PP)**
2. Then find the **subjects (S)** and the **verbs (V)**.

Some students, however, prefer to find the **subjects (S)** and the **verbs (V)** first. Each student, of course, should do whatever is more comfortable, logical, and natural for him or her.

The concepts here are difficult; you will need to keep repeating things like, "A word is a **subject** only if it is doing the **verb**" or, "A word is a **verb** only if it is what a **subject** is doing." Students need to be reminded of **Tool 15,** for example: though "study" in "to study" is a **verb** form, it isn't a **verb (V)** in this sentence because there's no **subject (S)** inside its **prepositional phrase (PP)** (or **infinitive [Inf] phrase**) doing it; though "practicing" in "when practicing" is a **verb** form, it isn't a **verb (V)** in this **sentence** because there is no **subject (S)** inside its **prepositional phrase (PP)** doing it. Students must see clearly that the **subject (S)** or the **verb (V)** can't be inside the **prepositional phrase (PP)** while its **verb (V)** or **subject (S)** is outside. This helps students see whole chunks or structures as definite and inviolable—this is an essential understanding.

Needless to say, at this point students are identifying **dependent clauses (DC)** as **prepositional phrases (PP)** because **dependent clauses (DC)** can be seen as using the tools for **prepositional phrases (PP)**. Again, what is critical at this stage of students' development is their being able to see whole structures, not to distinguish between **clauses** and **phrases**, which would be premature because at this point in their development students do not yet have a strong ability to recognize **subject-verb pairs.** This is necessary as a stage in their development. In Chapter 7, when students learn about **clauses**, they are easily able to distinguish between **phrases** and **clauses**, between **prepositional phrases (PP)** and **dependent clauses (DC).** Remind students that, as they proceed and as their **neural network** foundation develops, they will learn more and different tools about what they now are calling **prepositional phrases (PP).**

Students may have lots of questions. Keep to the tools for answers. And remember—the idea is that students are constructing **neural networks**; in the short time available they have time to learn only those things that are absolutely needed for expressing themselves in correct writing. If they want other grammar knowledge for its own sake, as noted elsewhere, they can take a pure grammar course.

Compounds are confusing, but they help students see structures. For example,

```
                             ─────SV1─────────          ───SV2───
S   BH1  C          ─BH2─  CV1   C   CV2   C   S    V       CVbl
He was and always will be jogging and running, and he loves swimming, too.
^──^──^──────────────────────────^───^       ^
```

This tool helps students see whole structures in sentences.

I-SG-WC: **Analyze** the sentences following: "Enjoying the autumn weather, she went outside to look at the fallen leaves." "Wanting to get good grades and full of determination to succeed, she decided to study a lot, especially her reading." (Always remind students that there might be several ways to correctly **analyze** a sentence.)

```
   Vbl                       S   V        ─Inf─  ────────PP─────────
Enjoying the autumn weather, she went outside (to look) (at the fallen leaves).
```

```
           ────────PP─────
  Vbl    ─Inf─              C      ───────PP────────
Wanting (to get good grades) and full (of determination)
```

```
──PP──              ──PP──
──Inf──    S    V    ──Inf──                    Vbl
(to succeed), she decided (to study a lot,) especially her reading.
```

CHAPTER 4

SUBJECTS AND VERBS 2

Again, it is helpful to begin each class (after the first day on a new chapter) with examples from students' previous homework to illustrate the use of the new tools.

Classwork 4-1, page 81

Here students are not being asked to guess the new tool; they are being asked to do the important **critical thinking activity** of processing their store of tool knowledge. Their getting the correct answer isn't important; their thinking is. This processing also prepares them to learn the new tools.

After the **whole class** debriefing, students will be eager for **Tools 23** and **24**.

Tool 23: Subject (S) and verb (V) are normally in the order of subject (S) first and then the verb (V) after the subject (S) (S-V). There can be words in between the subject (S) and its verb (V).

Students might want some examples. These can be written (without analysis) on the board for them to **analyze I-SG-WC;** for example,

They often <u>study</u> (at night).   We usually <u>worked</u> together.

Tool 24: There are some exceptions to Tool 23.

Two exceptions are in Chapter 4; five less common ones are in Chapter 10.

Tool 24a: Usually when "there" or "here" comes first, the order can be verb-subject (V-S) or helper verb-subject-verb (HV-S-V). "There" and "here" are never subjects (S).

Students need to know they have a choice. The teacher might write some samples on the board or the overhead for students to copy and **analyze,** for example,

A picture is there on the wall.	**(S-V)**
There is a picture on the wall.	**(V-S)**
There are some people working here.	**(BH-S-CV)**
Some people are working here.	**(S-BH-CV)**

Classwork 4-1, page 81

As usual, students work **I-SG-WC,** and their questions are the lesson.

Classwork 4-1, page 84

After the **whole class** debriefing, **Tool 24b** can be introduced.

Tool 24b: In a question the word order can be verb-subject (S-V) or helper verb-subject-verb (HV-S-V).

Students will benefit from some samples to copy and **analyze I-SG-WC,** for example:

Who is coming to the party?	**(S-BH-CV)**
Are you coming to the party?	**(BH-S-CV)**
Is Madeleine ready?	**(V-S)**

If it seems appropriate, the teacher might want to explain about the inflection used in English for **questions.**
   It also might be helpful if the teacher shows that when **questions** are turned into **statements** their **subject (S)** and **verb (V)** are sometimes easier to identify, for example, "Are you coming to the party?" **(BH-S-CV)** —> "You are coming to the party." **(S-BH-CV)**

Classwork 4-1, page 85

Students work **I-SG-WC** as before.

Classwork 4-2, page 86

Again, engaging in a **critical thinking activity** is important. After the **whole class** debriefing, students will be eager for **Tools 25** and **26.**

Tool 25: The second kind of helper verb is the root helper (RH).

Root Helper Verbs

can, could, did (**past**), do (**plural present**), does (**singular present**), may, might, must, shall (**future**), should, will (**future**), would

Note: "will" can be analyzed two ways:

Future	Future
—V—	RH RV
I will go.	I will go.
Both are correct.	You have a choice.

Note: Students will benefit from looking at the list of **root helper verbs (RH)** and their special meanings in the "Toolbook."

Tool 26: A root helper verb (RH) goes with a root verb (RV) to make a complete verb (V).

Students need to know that many **root verbs (RV)** are on the **verb (V)** lists at the end of Chapter 5.

Classwork 4-2, pages 87 and 88

Students work **I-SG-WC** as before.

Classwork 4-2, page 89

Students work **I-SG-WC** as before. **Tool 27** should now be introduced.

Tool 27: When a root verb (RV) has no root helper verb (RH) to the left of it and no subject (S), it might be a root verbal (RVbl).

The goal of this section, as in the analogous sections in Chapters 3 and 5, is for students to be able to distinguish between **verbs (V)** and **verbals (Vbl).** This is imperative because students' success at seeing **clauses** and **sentences** and, ultimately, at avoiding **sentence-boundary errors**, depends on their being able to recognize **subject-verb** structures. Their chances for success are better if they are aware of, and not confused by, **verbals (Vbl).**

   Students who know what **infinitives (Inf)** are might be given the option to **analyze** the **root verbal (RVbl)** as a **verbal (Vbl)** or as an **infinitive (Inf)** when appropriate. It is not important to make this distinction for the purposes of writing correctly. What is important is students' being able to see chunks of meaning or whole structures.

   Students will benefit from another example or two, especially ones that let them see several different verb forms in the same sentence, such as,

RH RV   CVbl   Inf or RVbl   RH RV

Stephanie <u>will go</u> shopping (to buy a toy that her <u>baby</u> <u>can play</u> with).

Again, before students reach Chapter 7 and learn about **dependent clauses (DC)**, it is premature and counterproductive to distinguish between **dependent clauses (DC)** and **prepositional phrases (PP).** What is important is their seeing whole chunks of meaning or whole structures.

Classwork 4-3, page 91

After the **whole class** debriefing, students will be eager for **Tool 28.**

Tool 28: When giving someone a command or a request, the subject (S) is the invisible "you" because "you" is who will do the verb (V).

Students would benefit from an example or two to show the difference between a **command** or a **request** and a **statement**, such as:

(you)V
Jeb,^ <u>get</u> there early.   <u>Jeb</u> <u>gets</u> there early.

Classwork 4-3, page 92

After the **whole class** debriefing, **Tool 29** can be introduced.

Tool 29: Sometimes when we give a request or a command, we speak or write to the person and use a name for him or her. This name is called the "addressing word" (AW) because we are addressing the person. The invisible "you" is still the subject (S). Commas separate the addressing word (AW) from the rest of the sentence.

Before going on to the next activity, students would benefit from an example or two, such as,

AW (you)
Phil, <u>take</u> your books (with you) (when <u>you</u> <u>go</u> home).
     ^

(you)   AW
 ^ <u>Take</u> your books (with you), Phil, (when <u>you</u> <u>go</u> home).
 ^   ^   ^

(you)   AW
 ^<u>Take</u> your books (with you) (when <u>you</u> <u>go</u> home), Phil.
                                                   ^

The examples on the following pages in the textbook will give students further practice in writing **commands** and **requests** and in using **addressing words (AW).**

Classwork 4-3, pages 93 and 94

Students work **I-SG-WC** as before.

Subjects and Verbs Comments

** Here is a very sticky problem and a typical incorrect analysis of it:

```
     S    V              ——S——    V        (—PP—)
   Peg likes (to hear the teachers read out loud (in class)).
      ^       ^                    ^
      ^____^                  ^_____^
```

The students won't have the knowledge to untangle this problem until Chapter 6 when they learn that "the teachers read" is not a **subject-verb** pair. They will learn to test structures in this position or pattern by changing "the teachers" into a **pronoun**; thus, the **sentence** would read, "Peg likes to hear them read" (and they will learn in Chapter 6 that "them" can never be a **subject [S]**). So let it go until then by telling students they will learn more about this type of **sentence** later. It is counterproductive to explain it prematurely because at this point in their development students don't yet have the foundational **dendrites** needed for fully understanding and internalizing this concept.

** I usually don't make a distinction between "shall" and "will" because "shall" is not commonly used these days. But if someone wants to know—and if there is time—a distinction can be made between the use of these terms for **first person** and **second/third person:**

I (or we) shall do it.   (ordinary statement of **first person** intention)

I (or we) will do it.   (emphasizes strong **first person** intention)

Everyone will do it.   (ordinary statement of **third person** intention)

Everyone shall do it.   (indicates a mandatory action for **third person**)

Chapter 4 introduces the **modal helpers** (here called the **root helpers [RH]**), the **base form verb** (here called the **root verb [RV]**), and the **infinitive verbal** (here called the **root verbal [RVbl]**). Naming these verb forms with the same word "root" helps students see they are related. Also, "root" is a more commonsensical and logical term than "modal" and a less cumbersome term than "base form." (If it were called "base helper" verb, it would have the same code as the "be" helper verb: BH.)

CHAPTER 5

SUBJECTS AND VERBS 3

We cannot overestimate how confusing and complex learning grammar is, especially now that students will be starting to put together the work they have been doing in the previous chapters. In this chapter students will also begin intensive work on proofreading. Thus, it is also very important now for students to understand that the purpose of **analyzing** is to find and correct errors in their own writing—not just to **analyze** for its own sake, which is a reason that **analyzing** the "Interesting Problems" should not be overemphasized or overvalued.

Students rate very highly spending five to ten minutes at the beginning of each class working alone and then with partners on finding and correcting the errors in the homework the teacher has just handed back, errors signaled by the teacher's check marks in the margin—one mark for each error of omission and commission in each line. After students have found and corrected as many errors as they can, they hand their corrected paper back in. The teacher's check marks are clues—a scaffolding—to help students develop their proofreading skill.

Chapter 5 is a good place to begin focusing on this proofreading activity because here students will finish acquiring all the foundational tools they need for recognizing all the forms of the **verb (V)**, arguably the most important and most variable element in a **sentence**. Students now need to develop their ability not only to see and correct errors in their **verbs (V)** but also, even more important, to identify their **subject-verb (V)** pairs. Being able to identify **subject-verb (V)** pairs is the absolute prerequisite for recognizing **clauses** and **sentences** (Chapters 7 and 8), which is the most important—as well as the most complex and sophisticated—**sentence-**grammar skill.

Throughout this chapter, as in the other chapters, students find it helpful when each class includes a few **sentences** from their previous homework written by the teacher on the board or the overhead for students to **analyze I-SG-WC** to illustrate and clarify the tools. Also, as in the other chapters, full discussion by students about their work and full exploration of their questions are the lesson. Attention needs to be paid, however, to keeping the discussion focused on the tools already worked on or currently being worked on. Other questions can be postponed until relevant tools are taken up or can be discussed privately with individuals if it seems appropriate.

Also, as before and throughout the book, the analyses are scaffoldings that help students gain strength in their skill and understanding. When students gain skill and understanding in their analysis and use of a particular tool or set of tools, the scaffolding for that tool isn't needed anymore. Thus, whenever an individual student has the ability to **analyze** and use a tool correctly, that student can be allowed to remove the scaffolding of the analysis for that tool or set of tools.

Classwork 5-1, page 101

After the **whole class** debriefing, **Tools 30** and **31** can be introduced.

Tool 30: There are two kinds of verbs (V): *regular* **and** *irregular.* **All regular verbs have the same past tense verb and prestarted verb (PV). They both always end in "ed." Irregular verbs usually have a different past tense verb and prestarted verb (PV), and they do not end in "ed."**

Note: Chapter 5 focuses on the **"have" helper verbs (HH)**, the **perfect** or **past participle** (here called the **prestarted verb [PV])**, and the **prestarted verbal (PVbl)**. "Prestarted" is used instead of "past" or "perfect" in keeping with the book's commitment to use logical, functional, commonsensical terminology: first, calling both the simple **past verb (V)** and one of the **participles** the **past participle** confuses students; second, "perfect" is not a commonsensical term; third, because this **participle** is used for actions that started in the past, "prestarted" is a logical term for this verb form.

Moreover, all the students will appreciate using a **tense**-neutral, commonsensical term for the main **verb (V)**; this obviates a great deal of the confusion that comes from their having to memorize and use an abstract, theoretical term, especially when that term also has a tenselike name that often contrasts with the **tense** of the **helper verb**. For example, the third example following, with its commonsensical, functional terms, is easily accessible to students. The terms in the first two examples, to the contrary, do not yield to a student's sense of logic but rather are nonintuitive terms that would have to be memorized:

1. She has done it for a year.   (**present helper** with **perfect participle**)
2. She has done it for a year.   (**present helper** with **past participle**)
3. She has done it for a year.   (**present helper** with **prestarted verb [PV]**)

If a teacher judges that it is important that students know the conventional terminology, he or she will find that students can learn abstract terms more easily and comfortably after they have first constructed a firm concept to which to attach the abstract term. And it is easier for students to construct a firm concept when the terminology is accessible.

Note: Some students, mainly ESL students, might know this verb (V) as the past or perfect participle. However, they easily accept the term "prestarted verb" because this verb (V) is always used for an action that was started before. Chapter 11 addresses tense in more detail.

Tool 31: There are four "have" helper verbs (HH). They go with prestarted verbs (PV) to make a whole verb (V).

"Have" Helper Verbs

have	has	had	will have
\	\	\	\ /
present	**present**	**past**	**future**
plural	**singular**	**plural**	**plural**
(except when		**and**	**and**
it is used		**singular**	**singular**
with "I")			

Note: Also to prevent confusion, the teacher might emphasize that the regular **past tense** and regular **prestarted verb (PV)** look the same—but that they are different because the **prestarted verb (PV)** must have a **"have" helper verb (HH)** while the **past tense** has no **helper verb**.

Several examples, such as the following, done **I-SG-WC,** will be helpful:

Past   HH PV

He played. (**simple past**) He has played. (**"have" helper [HH] + prestarted [PV]**)

Students can be referred to this tool in the "Toolbook" for a fuller account of the **tense** and **number** of these **verbs (V).** However, it is not recommended that the course focus in depth or in fine detail on **tense, number, person,** and **agreement** in the foundations section (Part I, Chapters 1 through 6). The goal is to get to the major structures section (Part II, Chapters 7 and 8) as quickly as possible so that students can have the maximum possible time to practice using them. Thus, the finer points or particularities of **tense, number, person,** and **agreement** are not presented until Chapter 11, which is included in the additional resource section (Part III, Chapters 9 through 12).

Students need to know that irregular **verbs (V)** must be memorized or looked up in the "Irregular Verb List" in Chapter 5. The goal is for students to become familiar with these resources and how to use them—not necessarily to memorize them. The more the students use these resources, though the more they will remember the forms.

If students want to know more about the meaning of the different **tenses,** the teacher might let them know that the class will focus on **tense** in Chapter 11. The teacher might also recommend to individual students that in the interim they study on their own selected activities in Chapter 11. The teacher might also want to interpose part of Chapter 11 in Chapter 5, keeping in mind, however, the major goal of leaving sufficient time to work on Chapters 7 and 8.

Classwork 5-1, page 106

After the **whole class** debriefing, **Tool 32** can be introduced.

Tool 32: If there is no "have" helper verb (HH) and no subject (S), then the word that looks like a prestarted verb (PV) is really a prestarted verbal (PVbl).

Classwork 5-1, page 107

This activity, **I-SG-WC,** helps students improve their ability to distinguish between **prestarted verbs (PV)** (**perfect** or **past participles**) and their look-alike **verbals (Vbl).**

The goal for this section, as in the analogous sections in Chapters 3 and 4, is for students to be able to distinguish between **verbs (V)** and **verbals (Vbl).** This is imperative because students' success at seeing **clauses** and **sentences** and, ultimately, at avoiding **sentence-boundary errors**, depends on their being able to recognize **subject-verb** structures. Their chances for success are better if they are aware of, and not confused by, **verbals (Vbl).**

Note: There are only three **verbals (Vbl): continuing verbal (CVbl), root verbal (RVbl),** and **prestarted verbal (PVbl).** Students need to keep in mind that what a word is depends on how it is used in a **sentence (Tool 4).**

Classwork 5-1, page 108

Students explaining their analysis of one of their **sentences** strengthens their conscious control of the verb forms.

Classwork 5-2, page 109

This is a **critical thinking activity**. The students' processing and thinking—reviewing and trying to use their tools—are more important than their coming up with the correct answer. This activity will prepare each student's brain for learning the new concepts and tools.

If students do not come up with the correct answer during their **individual** and **small group** activities, the teacher can write the two **sentences** on the board or the overhead and have the students walk through the analysis of the **sentences** as a **whole group**, checking with their tools:

> BH   PV
> Alice <u>was kissed</u> (by Reuben).

BH normally goes with **CV:** They were hiking.
HH normally goes with **PV:** They have hiked.
BH does not normally go with **PV:** They were hiked.

After the **whole class** debriefing students will be eager for **Tools 33** and **34.**

Tool 33: A verb (V) is called "active" when the subject (S) does the verb (V).

Examples done **I-SG-WC** will help students understand, for example:

    ————>   ————————>
She <u>hit</u> the ball.   The teacher <u>chose</u> him.

Tool 34: A verb (V) is called "passive" when someone or something else does the verb (V) to the subject (S). The passive verb (V) is always a "be" helper verb + prestarted verb (BH + PV). The someone or something that does the verb (V) to the subject (S) is always in a prepositional phrase (PP) starting with "by." This PP can be written in the sentence or can be understood and invisible.

    <————————   <————————
The ball <u>was hit</u> (by her). He <u>was chosen</u> (by the teacher).

    <————————   <————————
It <u>was written</u> today (by Jeff). It <u>was written</u> today.
                                 ^

                              It is understood that it was written by someone.

Students will benefit from doing a few other practice sentences **I-SG-WC**, for example,

                                   <————————
   ————————>   Passive
      Active   BH   PV
Harry <u>helped</u> Ruby.   Ruby <u>was helped</u> (by Harry).

                                     <————————
   ————————>   Passive
      Active   BH   PV
Pablo <u>read</u> that book.   That book <u>was read</u> (by Pablo).

Classwork 5-3, pages 111 and 112

One main purpose of Classwork 5-3 is to have students increase their fluency in having the correct combination of **helper verb (HV)** and main **verb (V)**. Students need to keep this goal in focus from now on.

Classwork 5-3, page 114

This is a **critical thinking activity.** After the **whole class** debriefing at the end of Classwork 5-3, students will be ready for **Tool 35**.

Tool 35: When three or four verbs (V) are in a row, any verb (V) that is between two other verbs (V) is both a helper verb (HV) and a main verb (V).

Students will benefit from having some problems to solve **I-SG-WC**; for example,

HH PV   RH RV/HH PV
<u>We</u> <u>have been</u> here.   <u>They</u> <u>will have seen</u> it.

RH RV/HH PV/BH CV   RH RV/HH PV
<u>Lee</u> <u>will have been working</u> a lot. <u>Amy</u> <u>might have done</u> it.

RH RV/HH PV
<u>I</u> <u>will have eaten</u> (before <u>you</u> <u>arrive</u>).

RH RV/HH PV/BH   CV
<u>I</u> <u>will have been eating</u> (for an hour) by then.

Classwork 5-3, page 117

This is a review activity. The teacher might want to use it as a test. But even if it is used as a test, students will learn the most from it if they have the opportunity to work **I-SG-WC** so they can help each other correct their work. By processing and doing **critical thinking** together, they all have a better chance of figuring out the correct answers and increasing their understanding of exactly what they are doing.

Classwork 5-4, page 118

This might be used as a review or a pretest. However, by thinking and processing in **small groups** and as a **whole class,** the students all will benefit from peer tutoring and will increase their understanding of **contractions.**

   After the **whole class** debriefing, **Tool 36** can be introduced:

Tool 36: Some subjects (S) and verbs (V) can be combined into one word by leaving out one or more letters. An apostrophe tells that a letter or letters are left out.

Subjects and Verbs Comments

** Remind students always to ask: What is this **sentence** about—"Who/what is doing/being what?"

   ** One of the most confusing and challenging parts of the course concerns the **agreements** of the following:

1. **helper verbs (HV)** and verb forms (**continuing verb [CV], prestarted verb [PV], root verb [RV]**)
2. **subject (S)-verb (V) number**
3. **subject-verb person** (Chapter 11)
4. **tense**
5. **referent-pronoun number** (Chapters 6, 9, and 10)

Students must become familiar with this material through continual practice with their own work so that this material is not learned as only rote knowledge.

** Frequently reiterate the good news that **subjects (S)** and **verbs (V)** are the hardest part of the course. After this, new concepts will be easier to understand.

** Students also need continually to be reminded that when they write they should first write what they think and feel; then they can match the writing with the tools and make any corrections that might be necessary.

** Students need to hear and believe the truth that as they continue to construct and connect their **dendrites** and learn the tools, not only will their first drafts begin to be more correct, but also they will be able to correct their writing more quickly and easily. But they always will need to use their tools. Every writer needs to do this.

The instructor might want to give a list of **idiomatic verbs: fall down, get up, wake up, pick up, cut down, roll over, tear off, come over, stand up, etc. Students can write these in the **Idioms to Remember** list. However, I prefer to present these idioms as **verb (V)** plus **preposition (P)** because then students can consistently use the tools they have.

** A point to be reiterated throughout the course is that the writer has to make choices. For example, the writer makes a choice about **tense** to get across subtle differences of meaning.

** After introducing students to the **passive-active** difference— which is mainly a **helper verb (HV)**/main **verb (V)** association problem—I drop the subject. Although it sometimes comes up later, I do not make it a continuing major element.

** Students will need to refer to the **verb (V)** lists frequently so they can use the correct forms. This is a complex, difficult aspect of the course—but as they practice, they will become more and more familiar with the various **verb (V)** forms.

CHAPTER 6

SUBJECT-VERB COMPLETERS AND PRONOUNS

This book uses the unitary term **subject-verb completer (SVC)** instead of the three terms conventionally used: **direct object, indirect object,** and **complement**. The purpose is to help students construct a concept for a structure or a chunk of meaning. This is more helpful to writers than their being able to identify discrete, individual elements that are important to theorists but not to writers engaged in the process of writing. As always, this book focuses on what students need to know in order to write **sentences** with correct grammar rather than on their learning theory-oriented concepts.

This approach also eliminates excess terminology and, thus, avoids the confusion students experience when trying to learn a number of new terms—especially before they have constructed a concept to which to attach the terms. This book's approach helps students construct the concepts needed for knowing how to write grammatically correct **sentences**. After students have a clear and firm grasp of a concept, however, the teacher can introduce the theoretical terms if he or she thinks it is important for students to know them.

Classwork 6-1, page 132

The first activity is a **critical thinking activity.** Students being actively engaged in thinking and processing, not finding the correct answer, is important. After the **whole class** debriefing, students will be eager for **Tools 37** and **38.**

Tool 37: After the subject (S) and its verb (V), ask "whom or what?" The answer is the subject-verb completer (SVC). Use your own sense of logic to decide what the whole subject-verb completer (SVC) is.

As always, the student's own sense of logic is one of his or her most powerful resources. Students need to learn to trust and rely on their own sense of logic. They will readily do this if the teacher reassures them of two things: first, they do have an innate sense of logic; second, there is more than one logical way to **analyze** some **sentences**.

Students will benefit from sample **sentences** to **analyze I-SG-WC**; for example,

Whom?/What?	Whom?/What?
^ SVC	^ —SVC—
<u>He is</u> ^ ready.	<u>She helped</u> ^ me study.

Whom?/What?

^ ─────────── SVC ──────────

We <u>saw</u> ^ the movie he <u>recommended</u>.

Note: Pronoun case is addressed in Classwork 6-3 and **Tool 41.**

Students will learn about **clauses** in Chapters 7 and 8; it would be premature and counterproductive to talk about **clauses** at this time.

Classwork 6-2, page 136

This is a **critical thinking activity**. Again, finding the correct answer is not the goal; the goal is thinking and processing so students can clarify and reinforce their previous learning and can prepare their brain for the new learning. This is also a review activity to help students see the difference between **passives** and **subject-verb completer (SVC) verbals (Vbl)**.

After the **whole class** debriefing, students will be eager for **Tools 38 and 39.**

Tool 38: The first word of a subject-verb completer (SVC) is sometimes a continuous verbal (CVbl) or a perfect verbal (PVbl). Use the continuous verbal for an *action* and a *description* of what something is *naturally in itself*. However, use the perfect verbal for a *passive description* (caused by something or someone else).

Students will benefit from working **I-SG-WC** on examples such as these:

SVC/CVbl

<u>They</u> <u>started</u> cooking.

^

SVC/CVbl

<u>He</u> <u>is</u> interesting.

^

A **continuing verb (CV)** must have a **be helper.**

This describes what he is (not what the **subject (S)** is doing and not what is being done to him).

SVC/PVbl

<u>He</u> <u>is</u> challenged (by the task).

^

This is a **passive** description because it is caused by something else (not what the **subject (S)** is doing and not what the **subject (S)** is naturally in himself.

BH CV   SVC   BH   PV

<u>It</u> <u>is interesting</u> everyone.   <u>We</u> <u>are influenced</u> (by her).

^   ^

what the **S** is doing: **BH + CV**   passive verb: **BH + PV + (by OP)**

Tool 39: The first words of a subject-verb completer (SVC) are never a subject (S) and verb (V). The verb-like word is really only a verbal (Vbl). There is one exception: when the first word after the verb (V) is one of these words, it might be a subject (S) with its verb (V):

who, whoever, what, whatever, which, whichever, that

Note: This tool is a main reason for introducing **subject-verb completers (SVC)** because without them students will be unable, in Chapter 7, to see why the following type of sentence is not a run-on: I saw the boats sail away. Chapters 7 and 8 give more information about this tool. Again, it is premature and counterproductive to discuss **clauses** at this point.

Working **I-SG-WC** on some **sentences** will help the students understand this tool. A challenging **sentence**, as the second one following, is stimulating and fun; even if—or especially when—students make mistakes, they are learning (as long as the example is not challenging them too far beyond their **ceiling level**):

$$\text{What?}$$
$$\text{What?} \quad \qquad \wedge \quad \text{———SVC———}$$
$$\wedge — \text{SVC—} \qquad \wedge \qquad \text{———SVC———}$$
$$\text{I } \underline{\text{know}} \wedge \underline{\text{who}} \underline{\text{won}}. \quad \text{She } \underline{\text{thought}} \wedge \underline{\text{that}} \underline{\text{was}} \text{ the right one.}$$

Note: The note for **Tool 41b** in the "Toolbook" and the note preceding **Tool 43** give a test using **pronoun case** to help students see whether the first **noun** of a **subject-verb completer (SVC)** is a **subject (S)** or not.

Note: In this chapter's "Comments" section, one other exception is mentioned. It is rare, but when it occurs it causes confusion; for example, "All we can do is laugh."

Classwork 6-2, page 138

This is a **critical thinking activity**. Moreover, students will benefit most from doing the analysis **I-SG-WC** first and then doing the writing of their own **sentence I-SG-WC**.

Classwork 6-3, page 140

This is a **critical thinking activity**. After the **whole class** debriefing, students will be eager for **Tools 40, 41,** and **42. Tools 40** and **41** are closely interrelated; it helps students to hear about **Tool 41** right after they hear about **Tool 40**.

Tool 40: A pronoun is a word that refers to a previous noun that is a subject (S), an object of the preposition (OP), or a subject-verb completer (SVC). The previous noun that the pronoun refers to is called its "referent." A pronoun's referent needs to be close behind it so it is clear what the referent is.
   (*pro = for, noun = a name; pro + noun = for a name*)

Tool 41 will provide lists of **subjective case (SC)** and **objective case (OC) pronouns**.

With examples, students will see that pronouns are used to write about the same person or thing without being repetitive; for example,

Marya told Mark what Marya had thought when Marya was at work.

Marya told Mark what she had thought when she was at work.

Note: Sometimes a **pronoun** refers to an entire **statement** or situation; for example,

The fire was burning out of control. It was a frightening experience.

The teacher can prepare students for **Tool 41** by providing them with problems to solve **I-SG-WC,** which will help them begin to construct their new concepts for **pronoun case (Tool 41)**; for example,

$$\text{SVC} \qquad\quad \text{SVC} \qquad\quad \text{SVC} \qquad\quad \text{SVC}$$

They like them.   She helped her.   You saw him.   He saw you.

We studied (with them).   They waited (for us).

Note: The term **noun** might be introduced here formally. It is easily understood now in terms of its functions as **subject (S), object of the preposition (OP),** and **subject-verb completer (SVC).** This can be done now because students have begun to construct a concept for **subject-verb completer (SVC),** the third of the three functions of a **noun.** By calling students' attention to the different forms of the **pronouns** used in the previous examples, the teacher will have both a helpful introduction to **pronoun case (Tool 41)** as well as some useful examples.

Tool 41: Pronouns can be subjects (S), objects of prepositions (OP), and subject-verb completers (SVC). A pronoun has a different form according to whether it is a subject (S) or not a subject. The different forms are called "cases."

Tool 41a: The pronoun when a subject (S): subjective case (SC) = I, we, you, he, she, it, they, who, whoever.

Tool 41b: The pronoun when not a subject: objective case (OC) = me, us, you, him, her, it, them, whom, whomever.

Tool 41c: Pronouns that do not change their form: either a subject (S) or not a subject = you, it, this, that, these, those, what, whatever, which, whichever.

Tool 42: When the verb (V) is one of the "be" verbs, a pronoun subject-verb completer (SVC) has the same case as the subject (S) (subjective case [SC]).

Students will need some examples to work on **I-SG-WC** to help them understand this tool; for example,

$$\text{SVC} \qquad\qquad\qquad \text{SVC}$$
$$\text{SC} \qquad\qquad\qquad\quad \text{SC}$$

It is I.   Who are they? (In a question, the word order is **V-S.**)

Note: Possessive pronouns are presented in Chapter 9, and **reflexive pronouns** are presented in Chapter 10. The teacher can introduce either or both of these cases briefly at this point—with examples to practice **I-SG-WC**—if she or he thinks it is necessary. However, being introduced to too many new concepts, tools, and terms at the same time can be confusing. It is especially confusing if students do not have the opportunity to do neuron/concept-constructing activities.

Note: Now that students have been introduced to **pronoun cases,** they have available to them a way to test **Tool 39.** Students can change the subjectlike word into a **pronoun,** as in the following examples. They will then clearly see that either the **subjective case (SC)** or **objective case (OC)** sounds better. Students need to know that a native English speaker will recognize whether the **objective case (OC)** or **subjective case (SC)** sounds better. ESL students who cannot hear which **pronoun case** sounds better will have to rely on **Tool 39.** This text appears in the note to **Tool 41b** in the "Toolbook."

RVbl
She helped her friends work. ——> She <u>helped</u> them work. **Yes!**

She helped her friends work. ——> She <u>helped</u> they work. **No!**

————SVC————   ——SVC——
RVbl   CVbl
<u>We watched</u> Jeremiah play the flute.   <u>He heard</u> the birds singing.
(him = OC)   (them = OC)

Tool 43: Every pronoun subject (S) and its verb (V) must both be singular (s) or they must both be plural (p) for number agreement.

Because **pronoun-referent number agreement** is less foundational than **subject-verb number agreement,** it is put off until Chapter 10 and **Tool 93.** However, if a teacher feels it is important for students to understand this now, students can be introduced to **Tool 93** and the related activities in Chapter 10.

Students will need some examples to work on **I-SG-WC** to help them understand **number agreement;** for example, students might be assigned to select the correct **pronoun** in parentheses in **sentences** like the following:

All the students need to buy (their) own books.
                              (his or her) own books.

Each one (needs) to buy (their) own books.
          (need)   (his or her) own books.

This type of **sentence** can also be a review of **subject-verb number agreement:**

Classwork 6-3, page 144

This activity might be used as a test. Whether it is used as a test or not, students will learn the most from this activity if they can work on it **I-SG-WC**, thinking and processing together to help each other and themselves better understand the **pronoun** tools.

Subject-Verb Completers and Pronouns

** Some students will not know how to handle **pronouns.** Listing pronouns is not enough. Saying that "**pro**" means "**for**" and "**noun**" means "**name**" and that "**pronoun**" means "**for a noun**" is not enough, though this is interesting and might be helpful. Saying that **pronouns** are used to eliminate repetition helps more. Here is another example in case students need it:

The students are studying. If the students do well, the students will succeed.

vs.

The students are studying. If they study well, they will succeed.

It is probably not necessary to take this point any further. The only purpose for learning about **pronouns** in this course is so that students can use correct **subjective case (SC)** and **objective case (OC)** and have **number agreement** of **pronouns** with their **referents.**
 ** Here is a **sentence** pattern that students sometimes use but that is very difficult to **analyze** before Chapters 7 and 8. If students come up with this pattern before these chapters, they can be asked to wait until they get to Chapters 7 and 8 to learn how to **analyze** it.

All he wants is to live in peace.

<u>All he wants</u> = S   <u>is</u> = V
          ^
DW ^
[**(that)** <u>he</u> <u>wants</u>] = **relative clause (RC)** (introduced in Chapter 8)

CHAPTER 7

CLAUSES AND SENTENCES

Everything has been a foundation for this culminating chapter. We cannot overestimate how confusing and complex learning grammar is, especially now that students will finally be putting together all the elements and structures they have been learning into **sentences** that are not **run-ons, fragments,** or **comma splices.**

Because this chapter requires that students do intensive proof-reading, it is essential that they keep focusing on the fact that the purpose of **analyzing** is to find and correct errors, not just to **analyze** for its own sake. Also, as before, full discussion of students' questions (answered by clarifying the tools) is imperative: their questions *are* the lesson.

To help students develop their proofreading skills, the teacher might want to begin class with two activities: 1) students work together and then with partners on finding and correcting errors in their returned homework, guided by the teacher's check marks in the margin (one check mark for each error of commission or omission in the line) and 2) students **analyze I-SG-WC** a few illustrative **sentences** on the board from the previous homework. And, as always, it is important to keep the focus on the lesson and tools they are working on or have already learned. (If the need for a new tool arises, create it and let me know!)

Classwork 7-1, page 161

After the **individual** work, **small group** interaction, and **whole class** debriefing—and the following suggested activities—students will be prepared for **Tools 44–47.** At this time the students,who have been **analyzing dependent clauses (DC)** as **prepositional phrases (PP),** will learn the difference between **phrases** and **clauses.** These first tools will make it possible for students to see the difference between these two structures.

It is imperative that students learn they can trust their common sense and innate logic—two of their greatest resources. Therefore, rather than merely memorizing traditional grammar rules, they need to practice using their tools as well as their own sense of logic in order to develop sensitivity to whether a **clause** can stand alone (**independent**) or not (**dependent**).

However, before introducing the new tools and terminology, it is essential to prepare students for them. As always, in this approach the learners begin learning a new concept by first starting to construct that new concept using their own sense of logic; then, when there is a concept to attach it to, new terminology is introduced.

Here is an example of a sequence of activities that uses this approach:

1. Using an **independent clause (IC)** a student has written on the board or one the teacher has written on the board, the teacher can ask students whether they feel it can "stand alone" or whether they want to ask, "So then what?"
2. Encouraged to use their sense of logic, the students decide whether the words on the board can stand alone.
3. The teacher can then introduce the term **independent** for a structure that can stand alone.

Note: It is important not to introduce the term **clause** at this point. The students first need to become familiar with the structure; then they can be given the abstract term for it. **Independent,** on the other hand, is a term that can be understood logically and commonsensically, unlike the term **clause,** which is abstract and theoretical.

4. These steps can be repeated with a **dependent clause (DC)**, either one a student has written on the board or one written by the teacher on the board.
5. Encouraged to use their own sense of logic, the students decide whether the **clause** can stand alone or whether they need to know more about it or want to ask, "So then what?"
6. The teacher can then introduce the term **dependent** for a structure that cannot stand alone.

After this initial stage of concept-construction, an activity such as the following can be used to introduce students to **dependent words (DW) (subordinating conjunctions)**.

7. Using the **dependent clause (DC)** from the previous activity, the teacher can erase the **dependent word (DW)** and ask whether the remaining words can now stand alone.
8. After this, the teacher can write that **dependent word (DW)** in front of the **independent clause (IC)** and ask whether this group of words can now stand alone or whether the students want to know "so then what?"

This sequence of activities can be repeated with **clauses** from other student **sentences** or from teacher-written **sentences** until the students feel somewhat confident about their ability to distinguish between an **independent** and a **dependent** group of words.

Students are now ready for **Tools 44–47.**

Tool 44: Clauses and phrases are two main parts or structures of a sentence. A clause is two or more words that go together and always has one and only one subject-verb pair in it. A phrase is two or more words that go together and never has a subject-verb pair in it. A phrase can be inside a clause.

Note: Students need to be reminded and encouraged to use their sense of logic to know which words go together.

Some examples worked on **I-SG-WC** will help students understand this tool; for example:

—————————-Clause—————————   ——Clause—— ——Clause——
——————Phrase——————
I drink water (after exercising).   I drink water after I exercise.

Tool 45: There are only two kinds of clauses: independent clauses (IC) and dependent clauses (DC). The only difference between independent clauses (IC) and dependent clauses (DC) is that dependent clauses (DC) always start with a dependent word (DW) and independent clauses (IC) never start with one. The subject-verb in an independent clause (IC) is called the "independent subject-verb" (ISV); it is the most important element in a sentence.

Note: The **independent subject-verb pair (ISV)** is singled out at this point as the most important element for one reason: it is a small, easily identifiable **sentence** structure that will invariably lead students to identify how many **independent clauses (IC)** they have in a **sentence** and what those **clauses** are. Being able to identify **independent clauses (IC)** is absolutely essential for knowing how to write with correct **sentence boundaries.**

For students who are just beginning to construct their concepts/**neural networks** for **clauses** and **sentences** it is easier to identify the **independent subject-verb (ISV)** structure than the possibly longer and more complicated **independent clause (IC)** itself. However, after the **independent subject-verb pair (ISV)** has been found, students can readily see the whole **independent clause (IC)** in which it is embedded. Thus, at this beginning stage identifying **independent subject-verb pairs (ISV)** is a scaffolding to help students construct their concept/**neural network** for **independent clauses (IC).** As their concept/**neural network** grows and students increase their ability to see **independent subject-verb pairs (ISV),** this scaffolding can be eliminated and students can begin to directly **analyze** for **independent clauses (IC)** themselves.

—————————IC———— [—————————DC——————————]
——ISV——Phrase–   DW   ——Phrase——
She likes (to study) [before her children wake (in the morning)].

—————————IC————— [—————————DC————————]
——ISV——   ——Phrase——   DW   ——— Phrase——
We work far (into the night) [when we have (to meet a deadline)].

As always, when beginning to construct a new concept/**neural network** and learning to use new tools, students will benefit from **analyzing** with all the codes and symbols. This scaffolding can be removed as they gain skill and understanding.

Tool 46: Identify a dependent word (DW) by these tests: 1) it's on the dependent word list; 2) when you ask "what?" after it, there is an answer; and 3) there is a subject-verb pair after it that answers the question "what?" Many of these words are also on the list of prepositions (P). The word is a dependent word (DW) or a preposition (P) depending on whether there is a subject-verb pair after it in that particular sentence.

Several examples worked on **I-SG-WC** will help students understand this tool; for example,

Note: The **dependent word (DW)** "if" presents a special problem that the teacher might want to ignore in this course. If the teacher wants to present it, here is a possible approach:

Tool 46a: "If" can be used for something that definitely isn't true and also for something whose truth we aren't certain about.

Is not true: If she were ready, she would be able to go. (but she's not)
              Use "if—were—would" together.

Is not certain: If she is ready, she can come with me. (It's not certain that she is ready; use the regular tools.)

Note: Students should be referred to the **dependent word (DW)** list and shown words identified with a single asterisk: they can be both a **subject (S)** and a **dependent word (DW)** at the same time. This is addressed in **Tool 64.**

Classwork 7-1, page 165

After the **whole class** debriefing, **Tools 47 and 48** can be introduced.

Tool 47: A dependent clause (DC) at the start of the sentence has a comma after it. A dependent clause (DC) in the middle of the sentence starts and ends with commas. A dependent clause (DC) at the end of the sentence has no comma before it. There is one exception: dependent clauses (DC) that begin with "that," "what," and "why" never have commas.

Using their **sentences** on the board and new ones the teacher creates, students will benefit from opportunities to punctuate **complex sentences I-SG-WC;** for example,

$$\begin{array}{ccc} & & \overline{}\text{ISV}\overline{} \\ [\overline{}\text{DC}\overline{}] & & [\overline{}\text{DC}\overline{}] \\ \text{DW} & -\text{ISV}- & \text{S DW} \qquad \wedge\text{V} \end{array}$$

[When <u>we study</u>], <u>we do</u> well.   <u>We</u>, [when <u>we study</u>], <u>do</u> well.

$$\begin{array}{cc} & [\overline{}\text{DC}\overline{}] \\ -\text{ISV}- & \text{DW} \end{array}$$

<u>We do</u> well [when <u>we study</u>].

Students will also benefit from the opportunity, **I-SG-WC**, to decide and explain whether and how they will punctuate their own **sentence.**

To help the students, the teacher might introduce the following useful aid. This aid can be used as a mnemonic device and a resource.

DC, IC   IC DC   I, DC, C

Tool 48: Most dependent clauses (DC) give extra information that is movable and/or removable. They can be moved to other places, or they can be removed from the sentence and the sentence will still be grammatically correct. However, whatever starts a sentence will seem the most important idea in the sentence to the readers.

Note: When a **question** starts with a **dependent word (DW)**, the **dependent word (DW)** is not analyzed as such and the **question** is not a **dependent clause (DC).**

——IC——   ————IC————-
Who <u>did</u> it?   What <u>do you want</u>?

It is helpful to use student answers on the board—or other **clauses** and **sentences** the teacher might write if necessary—to illustrate this tool. Students can **analyze** the **sentences** and then decide, **I-SG-WC**, which idea is most important in each **sentence.**

————IC————
[Before <u>it started</u> (to rain)], <u>they cleaned</u> the yard.

————IC————
<u>They cleaned</u> the yard [before <u>it started</u> (to rain)].

————IC————
My sister visited Europe [when she was twenty].

————IC————
[When she was twenty], my sister visited Europe.

——I——   ——C——
My sister, [when she was twenty], visited Europe.

Classwork 7-1, page 167

This is a **critical thinking activity** to be done **I-SG-WC.**

After the **whole class** debriefing, students will be eager for **Tool 49.**

Tool 49: There are never two dependent words (DW) like prepositions (P) in a row. When there are two dependent words in a row, each one must have its own subject-verb pair and one dependent clause (DC) will be inside another one.

Students will benefit from opportunities to **analyze** and punctuate **sentences I-SG-WC** with two **dependent words (DW)** in a row; for example:

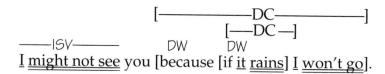

Note: Although some teachers might prefer not to include "not" as part of the **verb (V)**, it is included here because it is part of the chunk of meaning that is the **verb (V)**; it is what the **subject (S)** is not doing. As always in this approach the focus is on students seeing chunks of meaning.

Classwork 7-1, page 168

I-SG-WC as before.

Students will benefit from opportunities to move **clauses** around and to discuss—and improve their sensitivity to—the importance of placement.

Classwork 7-2, page 169

This is a **critical thinking activity**.

After the **whole class** debriefing, **Tools 50, 51,** and **52** can be introduced.

Tool 50: The word "that" is a tricky word. It can be used differently in different sentences. (See the list of tricky words.) It can be a subject (S), a dependent word (DW), a subject (S) and a dependent word (DW) at the same time, a subject-verb completer (SVC), an object of the preposition (OP), or a word that goes with another word (adjective [Adj]).

Students will benefit from more examples to **analyze I-SG-WC**; for example,

$$
\begin{array}{llllll}
 & & \text{[——DC———]} & & & \\
\text{—ISV— SVC} & & \text{DW/S   SVC} & & & \text{P   OP}
\end{array}
$$
<u>That</u> <u>is</u> that. I <u>know</u> [<u>that</u> <u>is</u> fresh]. I <u>am</u> grateful (for that).

$$
\begin{array}{ll}
 & \text{[———— DC ————]} \\
\text{—ISV—} & \text{DW}
\end{array}
$$
<u>She</u> <u>said</u> [that <u>she</u> <u>would do</u> it].

Classwork 7-2, page 171

After whole class debriefing, **Tools 51 and 52** can be introduced.

Tool 51: There is one invisible or understood dependent word (DW): "that" (except we can use "whom" for a person). The invisible "that" can never start a sentence.

Note: In the "Toolbook" there is a note for **Tool 51** that explains that English uses an **invisible** or understood "that" to avoid deadwood and that students can make their own choice about whether to use it or not.

```
                                                      DW
——ISV——                          ——ISV——  (that)
```
He <u>dreamed</u> <u>he</u> <u>was</u> president. –> He <u>dreamed</u> [^<u>he</u> <u>was</u> president].

Tool 52: After a mental action verb, usually "that" is the dependent word (DW) that follows it. Often it is invisible. Some mental action verbs are the following: know, think, dream, say, believe, understand, feel.

```
                                                      DW
———ISV——                          ———ISV—— (that)
```
She <u>understood</u> <u>he had done</u> it. She <u>understood</u> [^<u>he had done</u> it].

Classwork 7-2, page 173

This is a **critical thinking activity**.

Tool 53: If you can replace "that" with "this" without changing the sentence, it is not a dependent word (DW).

I know **that** man. ———> I know **this** man.
   Yes. Not a **dependent word (DW).**
I know **that** you saw it.———>I know **this** you saw it.
   No. A **dependent word (DW).**

Note: The part of **Tool 53** that says "without changing the sentence" is needed to help students avoid this mistake: "Yes, it can be replaced. I know this. You saw it."

Classwork 7-2, page 174

This is a **critical thinking activity**.
   After the **whole class** debriefing, **Tool 54** can be introduced.

Tool 54: When a sentence looks like it has more than one independent clause (IC), try to add "that" before each subject-verb pair. If it makes sense, then it is an invisible "that" dependent word (DW) and the clause is a dependent clause (DC).

Note: Later in this chapter students will learn about the different kinds of **sentences** and **sentence-boundary errors. Tool 54** is an invaluable foundational concept for that later section.

ISV?   —ISV—?   that

I am sure you know what to do.—> I am sure ^ you know what to do. **Yes**

      —IC—[————DC————]
             DW
   ISV   (that)
   I am sure [^you know what (to do)].

Classwork 7-2, page 176

After the **whole class** debriefing, introduce **Tools 55** and **55a. Tool 55a** introduces the first kind of **sentence, the simple sentence. Tools 55b** and **55c** introduce the other kinds of **sentences.**

Tool 55: There are only four kinds of sentences.

Tool 55a: If a sentence has only one independent clause (IC), it is called a "simple sentence." A simple sentence may have one or more prepositional phrases (PP) in it.

Note: At this point students can begin to drop the scaffolding of **analyzing** their **independent subject-verb pairs (ISV).** However, any students who have problems identifying their **independent clauses (IC)** should continue to first find the **independent subject-verb pair (ISV).** This will give them the scaffolding help they need to be able to find the whole **independent clause (IC).**
    Students will need examples of each of the kinds of **sentences;** for example:

        Simple Sentence
        ——IC——
     —ISV—
     We were there.

Classwork 7-3 page 176

This is a **critical thinking activity.**

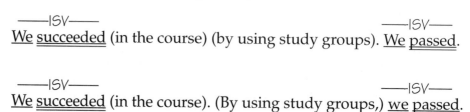

——ISV——   ——ISV——
We succeeded (in the course) (by using study groups). We passed.

——ISV——   ——ISV——
We succeeded (in the course). (By using study groups,) we passed.

Classwork 7-3, page 177

I-SG-WC as usual

Classwork 7-3 page 178

This is a **critical thinking activity.**
   After the **whole class** debriefing, the teacher can introduce **Tool 55b.**

Tool 55b: If a sentence has one independent clause (IC) and also one or more dependent clauses (DC), it is called a "complex sentence."

Simple Sentence ————Complex Sentence————
——IC—— ——IC—— [————DC————]
—ISV— —ISV— DW ————ISV————
We were there. We were there [until the library closed].

Classwork 7-3, page 179

I-SG-WC as usual.

Classwork 7-3, page 180

This is a **critical thinking activity.**
   After the **whole class** debriefing, **Tools 55c, 55d, 56,** and **57** can be introduced.

Tool 55c: If a sentence has two independent clauses (IC) and they are correctly separated (see Tool 56), it is called a "compound sentence." It does not matter how many dependent clauses (DC) there are (there can be none or several).

Tool 55d: Sometimes one or both of the sentences in the compound sentence are complex sentences. Then the compound sentence is called a "compound-complex sentence."

Independent clauses (IC) must be separated by an independent clause separator (ICS) (see Tool 56).
   Note: The teacher might remind students of the **compound** tools they have been using for **prepositions (P), subjects (S),** and **verbs (V): Tools 10, 11, 12.**

————Compound Sentence————
————IC1—— C ————IC2————
We went there, **but** the library was busy.

————Compound-Complex Sentence————
————————Compound Sentence————————
————Complex Sentence———— —Simple Sentence—
——IC1—— [————DC————] C ————IC2————
We were there [until the library closed] **and** it was busy all night.

This is one of the most important tools.

Tool 56: For sentences to be grammatically correct, 1) every sentence must have at least one independent clause (IC) and 2) all independent clauses (IC) must be separated from each other by one of the eleven independent clause separators (ICS): four marks of punctuation and seven words. These eleven independent clause separators (ICS) are the *only* ways to separate independent clauses (IC):

; . ? !	It is morning; the sun is up. It is morning. The sun is up!
, and	It is morning, and the sun is up.
, or	It will happen now, or it will happen later.
, nor	I don't like that food, nor do I like that beverage.
, but (must mean "however")	It is early, but they are tired.
, yet (must mean "however")	It is early, yet they are tired. ("Yet" makes the meaning stronger than "but.")
, for (must mean "because")	They went home, for it was late.
, so (must mean "therefore")	It was late, so they went home.

Note: In the "Toolbook" there are both the preceding overview and also a detailed description for each **independent clause separator (ICS).**

Note: "However" is never a **dependent word (DW)** nor an **independent clause separator (ICS).** (This often comes as a revelation to students!) Students need to be referred to the "List of Never-Dependent-Words" on page 203.

——————————IC1——————————ICS ————————————IC2——————————

<u>They</u> <u>went</u> (to the library)**;** however, <u>they</u> <u>couldn't find</u> a free study room.

                ^

<u>not</u> an ICS!

Note: Problems sometimes arise about the **dependent word (DW)** "so." For example, "so" and "that" (a two-word **dependent word [DW]**) can be separated by other words:

It was so big [that it didn't fit in the backpack].

Note: Also, "so" has different meanings with important consequences for correct punctuation; students can be advised that "so" is on the "Tricky Word List." The teacher might elect to omit this section on the word "so" if it does not solve problems students are having. However, here are some sample **sentences** that might be useful for students to do **I-SG-WC**.

–DW–
that
<u>She</u> <u>worked</u> hard [**so^** <u>she</u> <u>could succeed</u>].   (**Complex Sentence**)

–C–
<u>She</u> <u>worked</u> hard**, so** <u>she</u> <u>succeeded</u>.

("so" = "therefore"; **compound sentence**)

The following two additional uses of "so" are unusual and can be omitted unless students use these patterns and the teacher feels it is important to include them:

I did it, and so did he.   (exception to S-V word order, Chapter 10)
I did it, and so he was happy.
("so" = "therefore"; **compound sentence**)

Note: There will be more about **sentences** in the tools later in this chapter.

Students will benefit from **analyzing, I-SG-WC**, examples like these, trying to see whether they are grammatically correct according to **Tool 56.**

[———————————————DC———————————————]
[After he had called us with the good news about the new baby].
        Not correct

[———————————————DC———————————————
[When they went (to dinner with their friends at the Colony
——————]
Restaurant)].   Not correct

————ISV————   ———— ISV————
He had called us. Correct They went to dinner. Correct

Note: There are six exceptions to **Tool 56** (see following). These exceptions can be omitted if students are not using them, or the teacher might assign students to study **Tool 56** in their "Toolbook."

The Six Exceptions to **Tool 56:**

1. "Either" **subject-verb 1** "or" **subject-verb 2.** Example: **Either** it is **or** it isn't. (two **subject-verb pairs** with no **dependent word [DW]** and is no **independent clause separator [ICS]**)

2. Comparisons meaning more or less. Examples: The bigg**er,** the bett**er** (no **independent clause [IC]**) The **more** he runs, the fast**er** he gets. (two **subject-verb pairs** with no **dependent word [DW]** and is no **independent clause separator [ICS]**)

3. **Subject 1** "not only" **verb 1,** "but" **subject 2** "also" **verb 2.** Example: I **not only** work, **but** I **also** work hard. (two **subject-verb pairs** that can be separated only by a **comma**)

————SV1———— ————SV2————
4. With **quotes.** Example: "It is raining," he told her.
   (two **independent clauses [IC]** in one **sentence**)

————ISV———— ————SV2————
5. **Words alone (WA)** (see **Tool 62**): The job is, I am sure, the best one.
   (looks like two **independent subject-verbs [ISV]** in one **sentence**)

6. **Special expressions:** Thanks. Hello. (no **independent clause [IC]**)

Classwork 7-3, page 182

I-SG-WC as usual

Classwork 7-3, page 183

This is a **critical thinking** and review activity to be done **I-SG-WC**. After the **whole class** debriefing, the teacher can introduce **Tool 57**. This is one of the most important tools.

Tool 57: Dependent clauses (DC) do not matter when you are making sure a sentence is grammatically correct. Only the independent clauses (IC) matter. You may have as many dependent clauses (DC) as you want. But you must use this tool to be sure you have the correct number of independent clauses (IC). This is one of the most important tools.

Tool 57a: Every sentence must have at least one independent clause (IC).

Tool 57b: Every independent clause (IC) must be correctly separated from every other independent clause (IC).

Tool 57c: Count the number of subject-verb pairs. That's how many clauses there are. There can be only one independent clause (IC) on each side of an independent clause separator (ICS).

Tool 57 is one of the key tools that this course has been preparing students to learn and use. After this tool is introduced, students need to practice using it in every **sentence** they write.

The students are now on the brink of identifying and correcting all their **sentence boundary errors** and need many opportunities to use, talk about, and get debriefed on their use and understanding of this tool.

Classwork 7-4, page 184

After the **whole class** debriefing, Tool 58 can be introduced.

Tool 58: Whenever a sentence does not contain an independent clause (IC), it is a sentence crime called a "fragment." Correct a fragment by adding an independent clause (IC) to it or by joining it to an independent clause (IC) next to it.

—————IC—————— —Fragment—
<u>We</u> <u>went</u> every year. To the festival.   **Fragment Crime**

—————IC—————— ——————————IC——————————
<u>We</u> <u>went</u> every year. <u>We</u> <u>loved</u> (to go to the festival).   **Correct**

————————————IC————————————
<u>We</u> <u>went</u> every year (to the festival).   **Correct**

Classwork 7-4, page 185

As usual **I-SG-WC**

Classwork 7-4, page 186

As usual **I-SG-WC**

  After the **whole class** debriefing, **Tool 59** can be introduced.

Tool 59: Whenever two independent clauses (IC) are not separated by anything, it is a sentence crime called a "run-on." Correct a run-on by putting an independent clause separator (ICS) between the independent clauses (IC) (use Tool 56) or by adding a dependent word (DW), or by seeing whether there is an invisible "that" as an invisible dependent word (DW).

———————IC—————— —————IC—————
We <u>went</u> (to the beach) <u>we</u> <u>met</u> our friends.   **Run-on Crime**

———————IC1—————— –C– —————IC2—————
We <u>went</u> (to the beach), **and** <u>we</u> <u>met</u> our friends.   **Correct**

———————IC—————— [—————-DC—————-]
We <u>went</u> (to the beach) [where <u>we</u> <u>met</u> our friends].   **Correct**

Note: The **invisible** or understood "that" or "whom" **dependent words (DW)** can help students **analyze** their **sentences**. For example, a **sentence** seems to make sense and yet seems to have two **independent subject-verb pairs (ISV),** like in a **run-on:**

  -ISV-   —ISV—
  He is the one we like.

But how can this be correct? We know this follows the tool about **clauses** in that a **clause** is a group of words that go together and make sense and include a **subject-verb pair.** But this example seems to be a **run-on.** The invisible or understood "that/whom" **dependent word (DW)** makes it all right, saving the day! (In Chapter 8 students will learn the difference between regular **dependent words [DW]** and **relative dependent words [RW].)**

            [—DC—]
            DW
  ——————IC————— (whom)
  He is the one [^we like].

Classwork 7-4, page 188

As usual **I-SG-WC**

Classwork 7-4, page 188

As usual **I-SG-WC**

Classwork 7-4, page 189

As usual **I-SG-WC**
  After the whole class debriefing, **Tool 60** can be introduced.

Tool 60: Whenever two independent clauses (IC) are separated by only a comma, it is a sentence crime called a "comma splice." Correct a comma splice by putting an independent clause separator (ICS) between the independent clauses (IC) (use Tool 56) or by adding a dependent word (DW).

——————IC———— ————————IC————————
I <u>study</u> (at school), <u>it</u> <u>is</u> (near my home).   **Comma Splice Crime**

——————IC1———— ————————IC2————————
I <u>study</u> (at school); <u>it</u> <u>is</u> (near my home).   **Correct**

——————IC1———— [————————DC————————]
I <u>study</u> (at school) [because <u>it</u> <u>is</u> (near my home)].   **Correct**

Classwork 7-4, page 191

As usual **I-SG-WC**

Classwork 7-4, page 192

As usual **I-SG-WC**
  Two further examples are presented as problems for students to solve (**analyze** and correct). How can one decide in which **independent clause (IC)** to include the **dependent clause (DC)**? On the basis of what is true!
  Many such examples are needed so students can practice seeing and correcting the three crimes: **fragments, comma splices,** and **run-ons**.

S   V   DW   S   V   S   V   S   V DW S   V   S RH RV
We went home. **After we ate**. We got sick. He will **if he can** he will do it.

————IC———— —DC—— ——IC—— —IC— —DC— ——IC——
We went home after we ate. We got sick. He will if he can. He'll do it.

————IC———— ——DC—— ——IC—— —IC— —DC— ——IC——
We went home. After we ate, we got sick. He will. If he can, he'll do it.

Classwork 7-5, page 193

● This is a **critical thinking activity** to be done **I-SG-WC**.

After the **whole class** debriefing, **Tool 61** can be introduced. However, the teacher might want to omit this section and this tool. It is included here because students sometimes write **sentences** using a **dependent clause (DC)** as either the **subject (S)**, the **subject-verb completer (SVC)**, or an **object of the preposition (OP)**. If students do write such sentences, this section and tool are invaluable for discussing them. Otherwise, those correct-but-complicated sentences would seem to have been written without proper use of the tools.

Another option is for the teacher to inform the students that such a **sentence** is correct but that there is not enough time to study the tool for it in class. Students who are interested might be referred to section 7-5 in the book and to **Tool 61** in the "Toolbook" to study on their own or with their study partners.

Tool 61: A dependent clause (DC) can be a subject (S), a part of an object of the preposition (OP), or a subject-verb completer (SVC). When a dependent clause (DC) is used this way, it does not have commas around it.

Students will benefit from examples to **analyze I-SG-WC**; for example,

[———DC/S———] —V— [———————DC/SVC———————]
[What happens here] will affect [what will happen (in other places)].

[———DC/S———]   whom?   [——DC——]
                       P ^———OP———
[Whoever comes (to their house)] feels (like ^a person [who is special]).

Classwork 7-6, page 195

This is a **critical thinking activity**.

After the **whole class** debriefing, **Tool 62** can be introduced.

Tool 62: When a subject-verb pair is placed in the middle or at the end of a sentence just to tell what someone is thinking, saying, or feeling about what the sentence says, they are just "words alone" (WA) and not a regular subject-verb pair. They are separated from the rest of the sentence by commas. "Words alone" (WA) will always become the subject (S) and the verb (V) if they are moved to the start of the sentence. "That" does not make sense before "words alone" (WA).

—WA—　　　　　　　　　　　(that? No)
She is, I know, a top student.——> <u>She is</u> ^I know a top student.
　　　　　　　　　　　　　—IC—　[————DC————]

　　　　　　　　　　　　　　　　(that)
I know she is a top student.——> <u>I know</u>　[^<u>she is</u> a top student].

Classwork 7-6, page 196

As usual, **I-SG-WC** .

Clauses and Sentences Comments

** At this point in the course it is important that all the students try to write short essays rather than isolated **sentences** for homework. They can write in response to the suggested topics in the "Writing Practice" section. An option is for students to write in journals and then for them to select several **sentences** from their journals to **analyze** for class. I usually urge students not to do writing except for class and to **analyze** everything they write so that they will not reinforce their incorrect writing. I base this on the principles that what they practice they get good at (strengthen **dendrites** for) and that if they don't use it they lose it—and they want to lose their incorrect writing practices.

　** As students begin to learn about **clauses**, especially **relative clauses (RC)**, they are going to start writing very complex **sentences**—in order to practice their new grammar knowledge, which they enjoy doing, and because they now, finally, have an instrument for expressing complex thoughts and feelings!

　Some of the more adventuresome students—challenging themselves and exulting in their new-found power—will look like they have gone wild, writing hugely long **sentences**. Some may even forget to follow the rules in their excitement. Therefore, the word now must be control. Students will need to be reminded—and even exhorted—to keep their writing under control, that if they find out they can't **analyze** something, then they need to rewrite it so that they can keep it under control, can **analyze** it.

　They need to know that their thinking is still at a higher level than their writing skill. This means they can't yet express their highest level of thinking and feeling—because they just don't have the writing skill yet. Their writing level is rising step by step, and by the end of the term they will be closer to expressing their highest thoughts in correct writing. They need patience, perseverance, and practice to get to that point.

　** Students have many new **dendrites** and **synapses** in their brain; but, because these **dendrites** and **synapses** are new, students have to practice them continually, remain on guard, be careful to be aware of them and use them consciously—or else these new **dendrites** and **synapses** will disappear. This needs to be reinforced periodically.

　** If students have a problem identifying **clauses**, the problem usually lies in the students' imperfect understanding of **prepositional**

phrases (PP) and subjects (S) and verbs (V). By focusing on those structures and elements, they will better see what clauses are. One of the best ways to help a student who cannot see this—or any element or structure—is to ask him/her to explain his/her analysis. This will show where the problem is.

** Clauses can have other clauses inside them, for example: "When Jo, after Jim called, began crying, I helped her." Students sometimes write complex constructions like this, but they need to be able to analyze what they write to be sure their writing is under their control. Their power and fluency are shown to have increased when students can see chunks or structures so clearly that they can place clauses inside other clauses and know exactly what they are doing.

At first there will be confusion with analyzing dependent clauses (DC) that are inside other dependent clauses (DC). But students are at an advantage now because they have a dendrite foundation from the analyses they did with prepositional phrases (PP) inside other prepositional phrases (PP).

Here are some examples of a student's homework during this unit. The homework assignment was to write a complex sentence and then move the dependent clause (DC) around. He challenged himself to include two dependent clauses (DC).

** Numbering the clauses helps:

[DW1   S1   V1   ]
          DW2 S2   V2
She worked hard [because, [as you know,] she needs money].

[DW1   S1   V1   ]
          DW2 —S2— V2
He will fail math [unless, [as I myself found out,] he studies].

** This chapter introduces compound sentences and coordinating conjunctions, some of which have special meanings ("so" = "therefore"; "for" = "because"; "yet" = "however"). By this point, students should be clear that we analyze what is actually written down. If "for" is written down it will be either a conjunction or a preposition (P). But if "because" is written down, it can never be a conjunction, despite the fact that it means "for," which itself can be a conjunction.

** I include the comma with the conjunction. It makes everything easier. Students can draw a circle around the conjunction and then remove it and replace it with one of the other independent clause separators (ICS): the semicolon, period, question mark, or exclamation mark. As with everything, the more they practice, the more their neural networks will grow and the better they will understand.

** The regular in-class essays now might be done differently. Previously, students wrote for 15 to 20 minutes, skipping lines and then analyzing for the rest of the time. But now that they are learning about clauses and sentence boundaries, they need the opportunity to rewrite their sentences to correct any boundary errors. For this reason, these new directions are helpful:

1. Write for 15 to 20 minutes.
2. Copy the first **sentence** on another sheet of paper and number it "1."
3. **Analyze** it, correcting it if necessary.
4. Repeat with the second **sentence**. Then with the third, etc.

As usual, speed and completion are not important. Trying to have perfect control is what matters.

** For the rest of the term students should be practicing putting it all together, especially recognizing and correcting **sentence boundary errors**.

** Here is an especially confusing **compound**, which students can solve if they look for the whole answer to "what?" after the **dependent word (DW)**.

Again, they need to rely on their sense of logic.

$$[\underline{\hspace{2cm}}\text{-DC}\underline{\hspace{2cm}}]$$

          SV1   SV2
      DW   S   V   C   S   V   S   V SVC
[After <u>we read</u> and <u>we study</u>], <u>we feel</u> good.

** At this point, students might be making a number of errors. One reason might be that they have so many tools working at the same time that it is confusing—but if they study consistently and conscientiously, they will keep improving.

If a student is having problems, the best thing is to meet privately with the student, look at the homework, ask for explanations of analyses, and address specific problems.

** Sometimes the "to" of a **prepositional phrase (PP)** is **invisible** after this pattern:

All I can do is . . .
All I can do is (to try). —> All I can do is ∧ try. **"To"** is **invisible**.
All she wants to do is . . .
All she wants to do is (to help). —> All she wants to do is ∧ help.

It is not necessary to introduce this unless the teacher believes it is important or unless students are making a mistake with this pattern.

** Here is another type of problem sentence that sometimes arises; the analysis shows it is *not* an exception to **Tool 49** (two **dependent words [DW]** cannot be in a row for the same **dependent clause [DC]**).

As far as what they did, it was probably safe.

$$[\underline{\hspace{2cm}}\text{-DC}\underline{\hspace{2cm}}]$$

    —DW— SVC   —SVC—
[As far as what <u>they did</u>], <u>it was</u> probably safe.

"As far as" can be seen as a three-word **dependent word (DW)**.

CHAPTER 8

RELATIVE CLAUSES

This truth can't be stressed strongly enough and often enough: Students will not learn if they go fast. They will learn only if they go slowly and carefully, making sure they are doing it correctly. They are trying to grow and connect new **dendrites** in their brain; dendrites will grow only if students pay attention to every detail with carefulness and precision.

They want to go fast and soon be good at writing correctly—but they have been at this for only a number of weeks by now; their **dendrites, synapses,** and **neural networks** are not yet fully developed and dependable. Students must be ever vigilant, must pay ever strict, close attention.

As with Chapter 7, it is important for students to strengthen their proofreading skill, perhaps by spending five to ten minutes at the beginning of each class working alone and then with partners on finding and correcting the errors in their returned homework. This would be facilitated by the teacher's signaling the presence of errors with check marks in the margin—one check mark for each error of omission and commission in that line.

Classwork 8-1, page 209

This is a **critical thinking activity.**

After the **whole class** debriefing, **Tools 63, 64,** and **65** can be introduced.

Tool 63: Some dependent words (DW) are special. They are pronouns that relate back to a "referent" (antecedent) that comes just before them. They are called "relative words" (RW), and their dependent clauses (DC) are called "relative clauses" (RC).

Students can be referred to the list of **relative words (RW)** in **Tool 63** in the "Toolbook."

Sample **sentences** will help the students understand; for example,

```
————IC——— [————————RC————]
      Referent   RW
This is the book [that I wanted (to read)].
      ^————————^
```

Tool 64: Some relative words (RW) can be both a relative word (RW) and also the subject (S) of a relative clause (RC).

————IC———— [———————RC————————]
             Referent- RW/S
This <u>is</u> the **person** [<u>who</u> <u>wanted</u> (to meet you)].
            ^————————^

Tool 65: Sometimes the relative word (RW) "that" will be invisible. Both the visible "that" and the invisible "that" are correct. (Use either one as you prefer.) But the invisible relative word (RW) "that" can never be the subject (S) of a relative clause (RC).

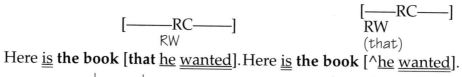

[————RC————]   [——RC——]
    RW   RW
                                       (that)
Here <u>is</u> the **book** [**that** <u>he</u> <u>wanted</u>]. Here <u>is</u> the **book** [^<u>he</u> <u>wanted</u>].

[————RC————]
  S/RW
This <u>is</u> the **lamp** [**that** <u>works</u>].

Classwork 8-1, page 212

This is a **critical thinking activity**.
    After the **whole class** debriefing, students will be ready for **Tool 66.**

Tool 66: Do not analyze a relative word (RW) as such in a question that starts with that relative word (RW). The question is not a relative clause (RC).

Which one <u>is</u> <u>it</u>?

Classwork 8-2, page 214

After the **whole class** debriefing, **Tool 67** can be introduced.

Tool 67: Four relative words (RW) have "case": who, whoever, whom, whomever. If they are the subject (S), they are in the subjective case (SC) (who, whoever). If not, they are in the objective case (OC) (whom, whomever).

[————RC————]   [—————RC—————]
  RW/S   RW
She <u>is</u> the **one** [**who** <u>made</u> it].   She <u>is</u> the **one** [**whom** he <u>called</u>].
  ^——————^   ^——————^

Note: If a relative word (RW) is both a subject (S) and an object of the preposition (OP), being a subject (S) is more important.

```
              [————DW————]
         OP/S
   I will go (with [whoever is ready first]).
                    ^
                    ^
                    ^
```

Subjective Case (SC) (**subject (S)** is stronger)

Classwork 8-2, page 216

After the **whole class** debriefing, **Tool 68** can be introduced.

Tool 68: A relative word (RW) that is the subject (S) of its clause must have the same number as its referent. Be sure to identify the correct referent.

```
        [————RC————]                          [————RC——]
     RW/S                                    RW/S
Those [who practice a lot] will do well. She is the one [who does it].
  ^____^                                           ^____^
  ^_____^
```

```
                                      RW/S
   The greatest success will go (to those [who practice the most]).
                                           ^____^
```

Classwork 8-3, page 217

This is a **critical thinking activity**.
    After the **whole class** debriefing, introduce **Tools 69** and **70**.

Tool 69: A relative dependent clause (DC) describes or identifies its referent.

```
        [———— RC ———— ]
     RW/S
Elaine, [who is my younger sister], works (for a newspaper).
  ^____^
  ^_____^
```

Tool 70: A relative clause (RC) must come immediately after its referent. When the clause does not come immediately after its referent, it is called a "misplaced modifier." This is a very serious mistake.

Students will benefit from contrasting examples like these:

Em has a dog who works here.   Em who works here has a dog.

```
        [——— RC ——]      [———RC———]
     RW/S              RW/S
Em has a dog [who works here]. Em [who works here] has a dog.
        ^____^                 ^___^
```

$$\overset{\displaystyle [\text{———————RC———————}]}{\underset{\overset{\displaystyle \wedge\text{——————————————}\wedge}{}}{\underline{It}\ \underline{is}\ \textbf{the laboratory}\ \overset{(\text{——}PP\text{——})\ \textit{RW/S}}{(\text{in room 51})}\ [\underline{\textbf{that}}\ \underline{has}\ \text{the best equipment}].}}$$

Note: A short **prepositional phrase (PP)** can come between a **relative clause (RC)** and its **referent**—but the meaning must be completely clear.

Classwork 8-4, page 222

After the **whole class** debriefing, **Tool 71** can be introduced.

Tool 71: A dependent clause (DC) uses commas according to where the dependent clause (DC) is. But a relative clause (RC) uses commas only if the clause is nonessential for knowing exactly which person or thing the referent is.

Dependent Clauses			Relative Clauses	
DC, IC	I, DC, C	IC DC	referent RC	Essential
			referent, RC,	Not essential

This is counterintuitive: **commas** needed when *not* essential.

Classwork 8-4, page 228

This is a **critical thinking activity**.
   After the **whole class** activity, **Tool 71a** can be introduced.

Tool 71a: If the meaning of the sentence would still be clear if the relative clause (RC) were erased, then it is just interesting, extra information and has commas. But if the information in the relative clause (RC) is essential for the meaning of the sentence, then it does not have commas.

Students might need help seeing the difference between the **sentences** on this page of their book. For example, they might not see that the friend's being a lawyer is not **essential** because all the friend will be doing is help build something. Being a lawyer is irrelevant and **nonessential** in this **sentence**. It is just extra, interesting information. But when the friend will be helping in a court case, being a lawyer is pertinent and **essential** for the meaning of the sentence.

To further illustrate this tool, other **sentences** will help. For example:

The woman, who is a doctor, loves to hike in the woods.
nonessential

The woman who is a doctor will give you some medicine.
essential

Relative Clauses Comments

** Here is a very challenging sample **sentence** for students to **analyze**. But, as noted before, the best samples for them to **analyze** in class are the ones you take from their homework—as they are or with changes you make in them to help reinforce their tools or to give students more experience practicing a particular tool.

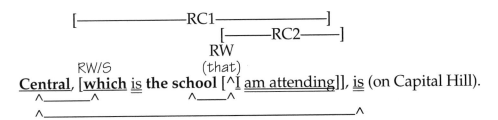

** Students have trouble distinguishing between **essential** and **nonessential clauses.** But by having many examples, especially contrasting examples, and by being able, as always, to ask many questions, they will eventually begin to see the difference. One of the most helpful aids is to emphasize that an **essential relative clause (RC)** tells us which specific person or thing the **referent** is and that if the **relative clause (RC)** were removed we wouldn't know which specific person or thing it is; for example, we can present the following **sentence** and ask, "What question do you have about this?"

The people went away.

Students will be able to see that they need to ask, "*Which* people?" We can then emphasize that, when we have this question, we need a **relative clause (RC).** When the students are asked to supply one, they will be able to do so.

For example,

        [————————RC————————]
           RW/S
The people [who were visiting here] went away.
           ^_____^

Students then need to be sure the **essential relative clause (RC)** does *not* have **commas.**

** Students have a problem understanding that **essential relative clauses (RC)** do *not* have commas and that **nonessential** or **nonrestrictive** ones *do*. This seems to run counter to logic:

essential = no commas

nonessential = commas

Many examples and reminders help.

CHAPTER 9

MORE ABOUT PUNCTUATION

Classwork 9-1, page 241

After the **whole class** debriefing, **Tool 72** can be introduced.

Tool 72: Punctuate compound lists of three or more subjects, verbs (V), objects of prepositions (OP), and subject-verb completers (SVC) by this pattern:

      A, B, and C   **A, B, C, and D**

Classwork 9-1, page 242

This is a **critical thinking activity.**
    After the **whole class** debriefing, **Tool 73** can be introduced.

Tool 73: When there are only two items in a list, never use both a comma and a connector (C).

        You, and I are ready.   **No**   You and I are ready.   **Yes**

Classwork 9-1, page 243

After the **whole class** debriefing, **Tool 74** can be introduced.

Tool 74: To see whether a comma should be used in a list, try using the word "and" instead. If the "and" makes logical sense, then you can use a comma.

On the beach we found a big and old container.
                            ^Yes
On the beach we found a big, old container.

Classwork 9-1, page 244

This is a **critical thinking activity.**
    After the **whole class** debriefing, **Tool 75** can be introduced.

Tool 75: If one of the items in a list has its own commas, separate the items with semicolons instead of commas or else the list will be too confusing.

On the beach we found a container, stones, and driftwood.
On the beach we found a big, old wooden container; a lot of small, round stones; and some large, interesting pieces of driftwood.

Classwork 9-2, page 246

After the **whole class** debriefing, **Tools 76** and **77** can be introduced.

Tool 76: Adjectives (Adj) describe or tell about subjects (S), objects of prepositions (OP), and subject-verb completers (SVC) (nouns).

Adjectives (Adj)
We found a big, old wooden container.

Tool 77: Adjectives (Adj) tell "what kind," "how many," and "how it compares."

four pillows   **how many** (four)
blue pillows   **what kind** (blue)
softest pillows   **what kind** (soft)   how it compares (soft**est**)
                           (the **most** soft of all the pillows)

Note: At the end of an **adjective (Adj)**, the letters "er" mean "more than another," and the letters "est" mean "the most":
That pillow is soft**er** than the other one, but this is the soft**est** of all.

—Adjectives (Adj)—
Here are the **two biggest wooden** boxes.
      how many^   ^   ^what kind
            how it^compares

Classwork 9-2, page 246

After the **whole class** debriefing, **Tools 78, 79,** and **80** can be introduced.

Tool 78: Adjectives (Adj) can go before the word they give information about.

Adj
She is reading an interesting book.

Tool 79: There is no comma between the adjective (Adj) and the word it is giving information about.

Classwork 9-2, page 247

After the **whole class** debriefing, **Tool 80** can be introduced.

Tool 80: Adjectives (Adj) can go after the word they give information about. Then they are called "appositives" (App). Commas must separate appositives (App) from the rest of the sentence.

————Adj————
The **wild and dangerous** lion roamed the jungle.

—————App—————
The lion, **wild and dangerous,** roamed the jungle.

Classwork 9-2, page 248

After the **whole class** debriefing, **Tools 81, 82,** and **83** can be introduced.

Tool 81: Adverbs (Adv) give extra information about verbs (V), verbals (Vbl), adjectives (Adj), and other adverbs (Adv). These words are always adverbs (Adv):

> **very   really   well**

> Adv   Adj/CVbl   Adv   Adv
> That **very challenging** course is really taught well.

Tool 82: Adverbs (Adv) tell how, when, where, how much.

> Adv   Adv Adv Adv Adv
> They eat faster (at home).   They are eating very fast now here.
> **^how**   ^   ^how ^   ^where
>   ^how   ^when
>   **much**

Note: Analyzing adjectives (Adj) and **adverbs (Adv)** will not help students write **clauses** and **sentences**. Also, **analyzing** a **prepositional phrase (PP)** as an **adverb (Adv)** or **adjective (Adj)** seems an unnecessary complication at this point in the students' development. An individual teacher, however, might believe it is important to have students **analyze** all their **adjectives (Adj)** and **adverbs (Adv)** and to identify **prepositional phrases (PP)** as such.

Tool 83: Adverbs (Adv) can go before or after the word they describe.

> Adv   Adv
> They are **quickly** finding out how easy it is. I am working **quickly**.

Classwork 9-3, page 250

After the **whole class** debriefing, **Tool 84** can be introduced.

Tool 84: When writers want to tell exactly what someone said, they put quotation marks around the exact words that were said. Commas and periods are always to the left of the quotation marks.

> He shouted, "Wait for me!"

If a writer doesn't use the exact words, quotation marks are *not* used. This is called a "paraphrase."

> He yelled at us to wait for him.

Classwork 9-4, page 254

After the **whole class** debriefing, **Tool 85** can be introduced.

Tool 85: There are three steps to spelling a possessive word correctly:

1. **Write down the correct singular (s) or plural (p) spelling of the word that is the *possessor* of the next word.**

The Possessor Word	What the Possessor Possesses
cat (**singular**)	collar
several cats (**plural**)	ears
boss (**singular**)	office
all the bosses (**plural**)	papers
Sasha Gonchovas (**singular**)	backpack
all the Gonchovases (**plural**)	summer home
pencil (**singular**)	point
two pencils (**plural**)	points

2. **Add an apostrophe + "s" ('s) to the end of the possessor word:**

The Possessor Word	What the Possessor Possesses
cat's	collar
several cats's	ears
boss's	office
all the bosses's	papers
Sasha Gonchovas's	backpack
all the Gonchovases's	summer home
pencil's	point
two pencils's	points

3. **If there is more than one "s," erase the last "s." You now have the correct possessive spelling. (There are two different correct styles. This is one of them.)**

The Possessor Word	What the Possessor Possesses
cat's	collar
several cats'	ears
boss'	office
all the bosses'	papers
Sasha Gonchovas'	backpack
all the Gonchovases'	summer home
pencil's	point
two pencils'	points

Refer students to other examples in **Tool 85** in the "Toolbook."

Classwork 9-5, page 258

● After the **whole class** debriefing, **Tool 86, 87, and 88** can be introduced.

Tool 86: Some pronouns are used for possession. Some possessive pronouns can never be used alone, and some can be used alone:

Never Alone	Used Alone		
my	mine	My work is done.	Mine is done.
our	ours	Our work is done.	Ours is done.
your	yours	Your work is done.	Yours is done.
	his	His work is done.	His is done.
her	hers	Her work is done.	Hers is done.
its		Its work is done.	
their	theirs	Their work is done.	Theirs is done.
	whose	Whose work is done?	Whose is done?

Students can be referred to other examples for **Tool 86** in the "Toolbook."

Tool 87: Possessive pronouns never use an apostrophe: yours, his, hers, its, theirs.

Its shadow was fading.   Theirs are late.

● Yours works the best. (If only *one* of your things works the best.)

Yours work the best. (If *more than one* of your things works the best.)

His writing was improving. Hers was also improving.

Classwork 9-6, page 260

This activity can be used as a review or a test. In any case, when students process it **I-SG-WC** they will be learning.
    After the **whole class** debriefing, **Tool 88** can be introduced.

Tool 88: Apostrophes are used for only three purposes:

Tool 88a: in contractions: you are —> you're

Tool 88b: for possession (except pronoun possessives; see Tools 86 and 87): Bob's movie, the babies' toys,

Tool 88c: for plurals of nonwords: She got three A's last term.

● Classwork 9-7, page 262

After the **whole class** debriefing, **Tools 89a, 89b, 89c, 89d, and 89e** can be introduced.

Tool 89: Words end in "s" for only five reasons:

Tool 89a: The word is normally spelled with an "s" at the end: yes, guess.

Tool 89b: Almost every present tense verb (V) with a singular (s) subject (S) that is not "I" or "you" ends in "s."(Root helper verbs (RH) do not end in "s" except "does.") Also see Tools 18 and 96.

Present	**Present**
He moves from place to place.	She writes well.

Tool 89c: When the verb (V) is the "be" verb, it ends in "s" in the past tense when the subject (S) is any singular (s) subject (S) except "you."

Past	**Past**
I was ready.	He was there.

Tool 89d: Many singular (s) nouns become plural (p) when we add an "s," "es," or "ies":

s	p	s	p	s	p
page —> pages		dish —> dishes		money —> monies	

Note: Students will need to use a dictionary to see which words need "s," "es," or "ies" (or a different spelling of a word) to make them a **plural**.

Tool 89e: Possessive words (except pronouns) usually end in "s" (see Tools 85 and 87):

the writer's book   all the writers' books   his book

MORE ABOUT SUBJECT-VERB ORDER AND PRONOUNS

Classwork 10-1, page 270

After the **whole class** debriefing, students will be ready for **Tool 90** and **90a.**

Tool 90: There are four more exceptions to the normal word order of S-V.

Tool 90a: The normal word order of subject-verb (SV) is reversed often after "not . . . , nor" and "not . . . , and neither." Be sure to include the comma.

Students will benefit from some examples to **analyze I-SG-WC**; for example,

S HV   V   V S

Kenny is not working, and neither is Bill.

S HV   V   HV S V Vbl

We didn't do it, nor do we plan (to do it).

Classwork 10-1, page 273

After the **whole class** debriefing, **Tool 90b** can be introduced.

Tool 90b: The normal word order of subject-verb (SV) is usually reversed after "not only." A comma (or comma plus "but") must come before a second subject-verb (SV). You may choose to add "also" to the second part.

V S   S V   CVbl

Not only is it easy, it is also interesting.

Not only is it easy, but it is also interesting.

Classwork 10-1, page 275

After the **whole class** debriefing, **Tool 90c** can be introduced.

Tool 90c: After ", and so" the word order is verb-subject (V-S)— but only when the parts before and after ", and so" are saying that the two subjects (S) did the same thing. The comma is part of this tool.

Students will benefit from samples to **analyze**; for example,

$$\underset{\text{They}}{\overset{S}{}}\ \underset{\text{ordered}}{\overset{V}{}}\ \text{a pizza, and so}\ \underset{\text{did}}{\overset{V}{}}\ \underset{\text{we}}{\overset{S}{}}.$$

They <u>ordered</u> a pizza, and so <u>did</u> <u>we</u>.
       ∧∧∧∧∧∧

<u>My grandmother</u> <u>loved</u> (to write), and so <u>do</u> <u>I</u>.
                                          ∧∧∧∧∧∧

Note: Students can be referred to the note for this tool in the "Toolbook" (", and" can be replaced by a **semicolon** or a **period**).

Classwork 10-1, page 278

After the **whole class** debriefing, **Tool 90d** can be introduced.

Tool 90d: Sometimes when a prepositional phrase (PP) is in front, the word order can be V-S or HV-S-V.

Note: The teacher might point out that writers put the **prepositional phrase (PP)** first when they want to emphasize the information in the **prepositional phrase (PP)** and also that this exception is used relatively rarely.

Some samples on the board to analyze **I-SG-WC** will help students; for example,

(Into the auditorium) <u>marched</u> <u>the graduates</u>.

<u>The graduates</u> <u>marched</u> (into the auditorium).

Classwork 10-2, page 280

After the **whole class** debriefing, **Tool 91** can be introduced.

Tool 91: Self-referring case (SRC) pronouns are used to emphasize whom the writer is referring to or to say that a noun is doing something for himself, herself, itself, themselves, etc.

SRC   SRC
She wrote it (for herself).   They themselves were the ones.

Students can study the list of **self-referring pronouns** in **Tool 91** in the "Toolbook."

Classwork 10-2, page 281

After the **whole class** debriefing, **Tools 92 and 93** can be introduced.

Tool 92: Some pronouns are always singular (s). Other pronouns are always plural (p). And other pronouns can be singular (s) or plural (p) depending on the sentence.

RW/S
————Plural————————Plural
They are the people [who speak (at every meeting)].
∧———————————∧————————∧

RW/S
————Singular————Singular
She is the person [who speaks (at every meeting)].
∧———————————∧——————∧

S
Who did it? (could be one person or many people)

Students can study the lists of these types of **pronouns** in **Tool 92** in the "Toolbook."

Tool 93: A pronoun must always have the same number as its referent.

The following examples can be used as in-class work or as a test. In either case, students will benefit most from processing these problems **I-SG-WC**.

Everyone should do (their) own work.
                                    (his or her)
    Singular   -Singular-
    Everyone should do his or her own work.
        ∧———————————————∧————————∧

He is the only one of the students who studies a lot.

Singular   -Singular-
<u>He</u> <u>is</u> the only one (of the students) [who <u>studies</u> a lot].
  ^_____^_____^

Only he studies a lot.

He is one of the students who study a lot.

<u>He</u> <u>is</u> one (of the students who <u>study</u> a lot).
         ^_____^

CHAPTER 11

MORE ABOUT SUBJECTS AND VERBS

This chapter, especially section 11-3, takes a highly detailed approach to the most complex element in the **sentence,** the **verb (V).** This might be a level of detail that exceeds the teacher's view of what is needed or appropriate. Some parts of this chapter might be used during the course as they seem appropriate, while other parts might not be used at all. Also, assignments to do specific sections or pages might be given to individual students as needed. All students, however, might be referred to **Tool 102** for a complete description of the twelve common **tenses** and a **timeline.**

Review, page 290

These problems will require students to be very careful. In the first problem the analysis is correct, but the word "ourself" is incorrect; however, in the second problem the words are correct, but "ourselves" is **self-referring case (SRC)** and not **subjective case (SC).** By processing their answers in **small groups** and as a **whole class** the students will improve and reinforce their knowledge and also their metacognitive awareness of the need to be careful and precise.

Classwork 11-1, page 292

The teacher might begin this section by drawing a **grammar box** with the terms **number, singular, plural, person, first, second, third, tense,** and **present** and then walk through the **grammar box** analysis of a regular **verb (V)** in the **present tense,** explaining each term along the way; for example, **first person** means "I" or "we."

The **notes** at the beginning of the tools for Chapter 11 in the "Toolbook" remind students of the foundational tool for **number (Tool 18)** and for words that end in "s" (**Tool 89**). **Tool 96** in this chapter takes it a step further.

After the whole class debriefing, **Tools 94, 95,** and **96** can be introduced.

Tool 94: Every subject (S) has person. This means the subject (S) is either first person (1) (I, we), second person (2) (you), or third person (3) (he, she, it, they); third person [3] is also everyone and everything that is not "I," "we," "you."

Note: A **compound subject (cS)** that includes "I" is always first person plural (1p).

——————cS/1p——————   1p
Joyce, Emily, and I love music.   We love music.

Tool 95: The verb (V) must have the same person as its subject (S). This is called "agreement of person."

Tool 96: Almost every verb (V) in the third singular (3s) present has "s," "es," or "ies" at the end. The root helper verbs (RH), however, do not end in "s" except "does."

Students can be reminded of **Tool 18** for an explanation of the concepts of **number** and **number agreement**. They already know the **present, past,** and **future tenses**.

Students then do the individual activity **I-SG-WC**.

If it seems appropriate, students might be assigned to create **grammar boxes** for other **verbs (V), I-SG-WC,** to increase their familiarity with these concepts and terms and their interrelationships. To help students increase their fluency in using these concepts and terms, they might be given an in-class quiz with time to process each answer one at a time, **I-SG-WC**. In this way students will increase their skill from one question to the next; for example, for the **verb (V)** "think":

What is the **first person plural (1p) present?**
What is the **third person singular (3p) present?**
What **number, person,** and **tense** is "He thinks"?
What is **first person singular (1s) past?**
What **number, person,** and **tense** is "You thought"?
What **number, person,** and **tense** is "We will think"?
What is **third person plural (3p) future?**
What **number, person,** and **tense** is "They think"?

Students will benefit from some examples to **analyze**:

3s   3s   3p   3p
He studies here.   They study there.

1p   1p   3s   3s
We work a lot.   She works very hard.

Students will now be ready for **Tools 97** and **98,** which are about **tense,** the most detail-heavy element in a **sentence.**

Tool 97: A verb's (V) tense tells when the verb (V) happens: present tense for verbs (V) that happen usually or always, past tense for verbs (V) that happened before, future tense for verbs (V) that will happen later.

Students can be referred to **Tool 97** in the "Toolbook" for **grammar boxes** for these first three **tenses**.

Students will benefit from some examples to **analyze;** for example,

Tool 98: Verbs (V) that happen at the *same time* must have the *same* tense. If they happen at different times, they must have *different* tenses. This is called "tense agreement."

Present   Past   –Future–
They <u>take</u> a trip every year. Yesterday <u>we ate</u> out. <u>He</u> <u>will call</u> later.

Students will benefit from some examples to **analyze**:

Present   Present   Present (that) Past
<u>They</u> <u>like</u> it [when <u>it</u> <u>rains</u>]. <u>We</u> <u>know</u> [^ <u>he</u> <u>won</u> yesterday].

Present   Present   Past   Past
<u>I</u> <u>think</u> [that <u>you</u> <u>are</u> smart]. [When <u>I</u> <u>went</u> to Texas], <u>I</u> <u>visited</u> Gene.

Classwork 11-1, page 299

After students process this activity **I-SG-WC**, they will be ready for **Tool 99.**

Tool 99: The "be" verb is the most irregular verb (V) in English (see Tools 16 and 17). There are three different forms for the present tense (am, is, are). Also, "be" is the only verb (V) that has two forms for the singular (s) past (was, were).

Students can be referred to the **grammar boxes** for **Tool 99** in the "Toolbook."

Classwork 11-2, page 300

After the **whole class** debriefing, students will be ready for **Tool 100.**

Tool 100: In a compound subject (cS) with "or" as the connector (C), the number of the verb (V) is singular (s) or plural (p) based on the number of the last subject (S) before the verb (V).

Students will benefit from examples to **analyze, I-SG-WC:**

```
——S—— V              ——S—— V
3p C 3s  3s           3s C 3p  3p
They or he does it.   He or they do it.
     ^                    ^
```

Classwork 11-3, page 301

After the **whole class** debriefing, students will be ready for **Tool 101.**

Tool 101: To name the tense of a verb (V) with more than one part, name the tense of the helper verb (V) (past, present, or

future). (Root helpers (RH) have no tense except for the follow-ing: did, do, does, shall, will. See Tool 101g.) Then name the main verb (V) continuing (CV) or prestarted (PV). Root verbs (RV) do not have a tense name).

Students can be referred to **Tool 101** and **Tools 101a** to **101h** in the "Toolbook" for a complete set of examples. A few **verbs** processed **I-SG-WC** in class will help students begin to see how to name **verb (V) tenses**, for example as follows:

Tool 101a. When you want to tell that an action is continuing to happen right now, use the present continuing tense.

> Present Continuing
>   BH CV   =   Present continuing tense
> She <u>is thinking</u>.

Tool 101b: When the verb (V) tells what was continuing to hap-pen in the past, the "be" helper verb (BH) is past tense and the main verb (V) is a continuing verb (CV).

Tool 101c: When you want to tell that an action will be continuing to happen in the future, use the future continuing tense.

> Future Continuing
>   —BH— CV   =   Future continuing tense
> I <u>will be writing</u>.

Root verbs have no tense.   =   RH RV
>   They <u>can think</u>.

Note: Students need to know that "will" can be **analyzed** two ways and both are correct. Writers have a choice.

> Future Continuing   Future Continuing
> RH RV/BH CV   —BH— CV
> I <u>will be writing</u>.   I <u>will be writing</u>.

Tool 101d: When you want to tell that an action started in the past and still happens, use the present prestarted tense.

> Present Prestarted
>   HH   PV   =   Present prestarted verb (V) tense
> They <u>have worked</u> there since 1990.

Tool 101e: When you want to emphasize that an action happened before something else happened later in the past, use part prestarted tense.

> Past Prestarted
>   HH   PV   =   Past prestarted tense
> She <u>had finished</u> her work [before <u>she</u> <u>went</u> to the gym].

Note: If that emphasis is not wanted, the **past tense** can be used:

> Past
> She finished her work before she went to the gym.

Tool 101f. When the verb (V) tells what will happen before something else happens later in the future, the "have" helper verb (HH) is future tense and the main verb (V) is a prestarted verb (PV).

Note: If you use a second verb (V) to say what will happen later in the future, use a present tense verb (V) in a dependent clause (DC):

> He will have practiced an hour [before class begins].

Tool 101g: Root helpers (RH) have no tense except for the following:

> did, do, does, shall, will.

The following points need to be stressed so that students can see that some **tenses** have subtle shades of meaning:

1. The **continuing participle** emphasizes that the **subject (S)** is, was, or will be doing something continually over a period of time.
2. The only use for "had" as a **helper verb (HH)** is to emphasis that a **verb (V)** happened before another **verb (V)** happened later in the past **(past prestarted tense).**

Classwork 11-3, page 324

Students can be referred to **Tool 101h** in the "Toolbook," either as a review or as an intensive homework assignment, according to the degree of importance the teacher puts on students' knowing the **tenses** and **tense names.**

Tool 101h: English verbs (V) have twelve common tenses. Each tense has a specific meaning, and writers must choose the tense that expresses their idea most accurately.

Students can also be referred to the **tense timeline** and advised to become familiar with **Tool 101, Tools 101a to 101h,** and the **timeline** because these can be powerful resources for them.

   It is important for students to struggle with the logic and meaning of **verb (V) tenses.**

CHAPTER 12

ARTICLES, VERBALS, AND IDIOMS FOR ESL STUDENTS

Chapters 2 to 11 will help ESL students express their ideas in correct standard English sentences. There are, however, some elements that give ESL students particular difficulty. These problems (articles, verbals [Vbl], and idioms) are addressed in Chapter 12. This chapter might be assigned to individual ESL students as needed. Alternatively, it might be assigned to the entire ESL population of the class as an extra assignment, with the teacher or an aide meeting the students for several extra study sessions outside class. If the school has a learning lab, a third alternative might be to assign the students to work with tutors in the lab, either individually or as a group. On the other hand, if a large proportion of the class is ESL students, this chapter might be assigned to the entire class. The native speakers, then, could act as peer tutors during the small group work, which could deepen and enrich their own understanding of English. If aides or tutors participate, the teacher might want to acquaint them with the Natural Human Learning Process approach.

Classwork 12-1, page 333

This activity might serve as a pretest.

After the **whole class** debriefing, **Tool 102** can be presented as a general introduction to articles. **Tools 103** and **104** will later present more details about articles. See examples in the "Toolbook."

Tool 102: In English there are three articles: a, an, the.

Tool 102a: Articles go before most specific subjects (S), subject-verb completers (SVC), and objects of the preposition (OP). If there is no article, there usually must be a word telling how many: one, ten, some, many, any, etc. (The book was new. She bought two books yesterday.)

Tool 102b: General things usually do not have an article. (I love books.)

Tool 102c: Articles usually go before a person's title (the doctor). **But they usually do not go before the title with the name** (Doctor Gabe, *not* the Doctor Gabe).

Tool 102d: Articles usually do not go before the proper name of a person, city, or state (Jill, Miami, Ohio). **But articles usually do go before the proper name of a building or a structure** (the Empire State Building).

Tool 102e: When a nation's name is actually just a description (the United States; what kind of states? united ones) **instead of a particular name** (America), **it must have an article.**

Classwork 12-1, page 335

After the **whole class** debriefing, **Tools 103** and **104** can be introduced.
See examples in the "Toolbook."

Tool 103a: "The" can be used for singular (s) or plural (p). Use "the" to mean "this or that specific one" (singular [s]) or "these or those specific ones" (plural [p]). This is called a "definite article" (definite=specific).

The library was closed. = This specific library was closed.
The stores were open. = Those specific stores in a specific place
were open.
The books are ready. = These specific books are ready.

Tool 103b: Use "a" and "an" to mean "any" or "some sort of." This is called a "infinite article" (infinite = not specific).

A library is an important place. = Any library is some sort of
important place.

Note: If it seems appropriate, the teacher might include the following point: The first time you mention someone or something without being specific, use "a" or "an." The second time you mention the same person or thing, use "the."

A storm was approaching.   By noon the storm had reached
full force.

Tool 104a: Use "a" when the next word starts with a consonant: *b, c, d, f, g, j, k, l, m, n, p, q, r, s, t, v, w, x, y, z*, and sometimes *h*—but only when the "h" sounds like "h" (a half cup, an hour). **This makes pronunciation easier.**

Tool 104b: Use "an" when the next word starts with a vowel: a, e, i, o, and sometimes u—but only when the "u" sounds like "uh" (an ugly storm, a useful book). This is also to make pronunciation easier.

Students will grasp this if they have the opportunity to pronounce aloud these and other exemplifying words with their **articles**.

Classwork 12-2, page 337

This section is very complex and detailed. If the teacher finds it too detailed, parts might be omitted. There is no way students can memorize or learn to use these tools in a short time. The tools for this section, however, can be a valuable resource for the students.

See the examples in the "Toolbook."

After the **whole class** debriefing, **Tools 105, 106, 107, 108,** and **109** can be introduced.

Tool 105: When a verb-like word comes after "to," normally use a root verbal (RVbl). This is an infinitive (Inf).

RVbl
I want (to write an article).

Tool 106: When a verb-like word comes after any preposition (P), except "to," normally use the continuing verbal (CVbl).

RVbl   CVbl
I want (to do a lot (of writing)).

Tool 107: Two verbs (V) are used in a row only when the first one is a helper verb (HV).

RH RV
She can find it.

If you write two verb-like words in a row and the first is not a helper verb (HV), put "to" in front of the second verb-like word and make it a root verbal (RVbl). Add "to" even when other words are between the verb (V) and/or verbal (Vbl).

Incorrect: She wants find it.
     ^ very much

RVbl

Correct: She wants (to find it).
     ^ very much

See details and examples in Chapter 12 in the "Toolbook."

Tool 108: There are exceptions to Tool 107.

These exceptions are complex and detailed. Students might be assigned to study these exceptions in the "Toolbook."

Tool 109: Some words are followed by "to" with a continuing verbal (CVbl), for example,

$$\text{CVbl}$$
"look forward": I look forward (to going).

Students can be referred to the other words and examples in the "Toolbook."

Classwork 12-3, page 339

An **idiom** is a way of speaking in one language that cannot be translated with good sense into another language. Also, there are no tools for **idioms**, which are numerous and which change over time. They must be memorized and practiced. The five **idioms** presented in this chapter are only for the purpose of introducing students to the reality and nature of **idioms**. Teachers might want to add other **idioms**; and students might be referred to any number of books of **idioms**, for example, *Essential American Idioms*, Richard A. Spears, National Textbook Company, 1992.

There is a section at the end of Chapter 12 where students can write down **idioms** they are assigned and also any **idioms** they want to remember.

Some **prepositions (P)** are used **idiomatically**. See examples in the "Toolbook" at the end of Chapter 12.

IN-CLASS
ESSAY PROMPTS

These prompts are suggested as topics for end-of-chapter essays to be done in class or as homework. The prompts are not in any particular order. Select whichever one seems most appropriate for your students for each chapter. You also might want to create some prompts of your own. These prompts might also be used as writing tests during the quarter and as the final exam. Students rate this type of writing prompt very highly.

Suggested Directions: Distribute a copy of the prompt to each student and read it aloud, making sure all the students understand the vocabulary and the task. Students then write for 15 to 20 minutes. After this they spend 20 to 30 minutes analyzing what they have written, correcting any errors they find. It is recommended that this be an open-book, open-note activity or test so that students can practice using their resources; the focus is not intended to be on their ability to memorize but, rather, on their trying to be correct and using all the resources available to them.

1. A baseball player from a poor family is eager to come to college and has applied for a scholarship. He has just barely made it through high school and would probably have difficulty with college courses. He would, however, be a great help to the college baseball team, which is badly in need of good players. Should the only remaining college scholarship go to him or to another student, also from a poor family, who has an excellent scholastic record but is not a baseball player?

    You are on the scholarship committee and have to help make the decision about who gets the scholarship. Which student would you choose? Why?

2. A widow who is sixty years old has been hit by a car. She is now in the hospital being kept alive only by a life-support machine. The doctor believes there is no possibility that the woman will ever regain consciousness. Her children, all of whom are adults with their own families, have begged the doctor to remove the life-support machine, which is just prolonging their agony over their mother. But the doctor cannot do so because it is against the law.

At this time the state legislature is thinking about making a new law that would let doctors remove life-support machines when a group of medical specialists say the patient can never recover.

If you were a legislator, would you vote for this law? Why or why not?

3. A spaceship lands, and the aliens, who speak English, ask you to tell them about Earth, the people who live on Earth, and what life is like here.

Decide whether you will tell about only the good things or whether you will tell about both the good and the bad things. Decide whether you will tell them about the past as well as the present or only about the present. What aspects of life on Earth will you tell them about and why?

4. You are studying for a final exam that you will be taking tomorrow. This is the end of your last year in college, and this course is required for your degree. It is a course that is very difficult for you. In fact, you took this course once before and failed it. So this is your last chance. Also, if you fail this course, you cannot take the good job that you have been offered.

Your phone rings. Your sister is calling and tells you her husband has just had a heart attack. She has spoken to the doctor, who is sending an ambulance to take him to the hospital. Your sister is very frightened and begs you to meet her at the hospital to stand by her. You are her only relative in the city and you two are very close. Also, she stood beside you during difficult times in your life. You realize, however, that if you do what she asks you will not be able to study for the exam.

Finish the story. Tell what happens next.

5. A married couple both worked, had a two-year-old child, a beautiful home, two cars, lovely furniture, and many bills each month to pay for all that they had. Then the woman lost her job as a top manager in a radio manufacturing company because the company went out of business. She had been a highly paid expert and had felt great satisfaction in her work. She tried to find work in her field but was not able to because many companies like hers were also going out of business.

She decided to go back to college to train for a new field so that she could use her talents, be an expert, earn a high salary, and get satisfaction from her job. She decided to go into the field of computers. But to complete the training would take four years. Her husband said she could not do this because they needed the money, and they couldn't afford her not working for four years.

He told her to take any kind of job because they had to have money each month to pay for their expenses.

She tried to get a job but did not find anything challenging or satisfying. She became very unhappy and began to lose her self-confidence. She told her husband she had to go back to college because she could not live this way. He told her, if she did, he would divorce her because she was not loyal to the family and was not carrying her share of responsibility for the family.

You are a counselor to whom they come for help. What is your opinion of these people and what do you think they should do?

6. Some people had to leave their homeland. They went to live in a different country with a different culture and language. Some of the people didn't want themselves, and especially their children, to learn the new language, customs, culture, and values. Some others thought it was good to learn the new language, ways, culture, and values.

Explain what is good or bad—or both—about one of these points of view or about both points of view.

7. A scientist who was an expert in genetics decided to do some experiments that would influence babies before they were born. She wanted to influence babies' physical growth and intelligence. She believed her work would help create stronger, more intelligent babies, which would benefit all humanity. Therefore, she was proud and happy to be doing this work. She believed the long-range results would be good and all people would benefit. One day she read that the government was getting interested in the work she was doing. She became afraid that if government agencies got control of her work, they might use it for purposes with which she would disagree. She remembered what governments had done with discoveries about the atom that could have helped people but instead were used for war. As a result she destroyed her work to which she had given twenty years of her life.

Do you think she was right or wrong? Why?

8. The college bookstore, where Liz works, has been losing many things to shoplifters; so the boss has decided to do something. Liz and her fellow workers have been asked to look for anything that they might think is suspicious. This morning Liz has been noticing that, whenever a certain customer bends down to a bottom shelf, he looks around. After watching him for awhile, Liz thinks she should tell her boss that this customer's behavior is suspicious. Because the customer has been bending down, Liz has not been able to see his face. Suddenly, however, he turns around

and Liz sees it is her friend. She decides she will not tell on him because she knows he is poor and cannot afford all the supplies he needs for school. She lets him leave, but afterwards she feels she should have been thinking more about the store than about her friend.

What would *you* have done in this situation? Why?

9. Some Europeans came to the American continent in the 1600s. They did not have freedom in Europe because their rulers controlled their lives. These Europeans came to America to have a freer life. When the Europeans landed in America, they found that people were already living here. These people were called Indians by the Europeans. The Indians at first had sympathy for the Europeans and were willing to share this land with them. As time went by, however, more and more Europeans came to this land because they were being treated very cruelly by their rulers in Europe and had no freedom. They needed more and more land. The Indians became worried that the Europeans were taking too much of their land and would soon take it all. When they said they didn't want to give the Europeans any more land, the Europeans used their armies and guns to drive the Indians away. The Indians fought back, but the Europeans had more powerful weapons and were able to take all the land. The Europeans created their own government and ruled over America. They gave the Indians only a few small areas to live in called reservations.

If you had the power to go back and make that history be different, what would you change and why?

10. You have applied for a job that is perfect for you. It is in the field that you have been studying and in which you have the most interest. It will be challenging and creative; you will be able to make a good contribution to society; there will be good promotions; and it pays an excellent salary.

You are one of three finalists. Each of you three finalists now has to meet with the company president and then take a test. The decision about who will get the job will be based on the interview and the test.

The other two finalists were your classmates in college. You know that they both do very well on tests. You, on the other hand, freeze up on tests and usually do a poor job. You are angry and upset that the decision will be based on a test. You think it is unfair.

You wonder whether you should explain this to the president and ask him whether there is another way to decide who will get the job. You go in for your interview. The president likes you very much and says he will definitely give you the job if you do well on the test. You decide to discuss the test with him because you are now hopeful that he will be understanding and will find another way because he really wants you for the job.

Just then the president gets an urgent phone call and says he has to leave for about ten minutes. He asks you to wait. He leaves. You notice two envelopes on his desk. One says "TEST." The other says "TEST ANSWERS."   What will you do? Why?

11. A required course in college had a reputation as being excellent but also very difficult. All the students who took the course were aware of its reputation. One reason the course was difficult was that students were required to write five long papers. Mike, a senior in college, took this course and wrote the first four papers. When the time came to write the last one, he had many other things to do to get ready for graduate school, for which he had won a scholarship. He had to write a senior essay, required of all graduates, and he also had to fill out many complicated forms for his scholarship.

One of his friends, also an excellent student, had taken this course two years before and still had his papers. Mike asked his friend for one of his papers. Mike rewrote some parts of it and handed it in, believing that the teacher would never remember a paper that had been written that long ago, especially since many people had taken the course since then. However, the teacher recognized the paper and even the name of the student who had written it.

The college's official policy for using someone else's work (plagiarism) was to expel the plagiarizer from school. All teachers were required to immediately report and expel any student caught plagiarizing.

If you were the teacher, and you knew that Mike was about to graduate and had already been accepted into graduate school with a scholarship, what would you do? Why?

12. I recently read a story about a Puerto Rican boy whose family had come to the United States from Puerto Rico before the boy was born. Even though the boy himself was born in the United States, his father had been born in Puerto Rico, which is part of the United States. In the story, the boy's father told him about a great hero of his country of Puerto Rico. This hero had said Puerto Ricans should never forget that their true country is Puerto Rico, which had been conquered and was still controlled by the United States. This hero said that he would never salute the flag of the

United States. The boy's father said he agreed with this hero. The next day at school the boy decided he would follow the example of this hero and also not salute the U.S. flag. However, he got into trouble when he refused to salute the American flag. The school principal finally called the boy's father and asked him to tell his son to obey the rules of the school. The father was afraid his son would ruin his good school record and his chances for the future, so he told him to obey. The son began to cry because he felt his father was a coward.

What do you think of this father, his son, and their story?

13. Mr. and Mrs. Winters lived in a lovely home in a small city in the Midwest. They had two children of whom they were very proud. Their daughter was a top student in college, and their son, who had just graduated with honors from West Point Military Academy, was a lieutenant in the army. They believed being in the army was an honorable career for their son.

Mr. Winters owned a hardware store that had been in his family since his grandfather first started it; he and Mrs. Winters belonged to a church, had many good friends, and participated in community activities because they believed people should help each other. For example, Mrs. Winters worked in the hospital several days a week as a volunteer, and Mr. Winters belonged to an organization that raised money for good causes like building new playgrounds for children or buying wheelchairs for disabled senior citizens.

One day the Winterses heard on the radio that a war had broken out between two countries in the middle of Europe because of a dispute over the boundary between the two countries. The Winterses thought this was a poor reason to have a war in which homes and businesses would be destroyed and, worse, people would die. However, they did not pay much attention to this war until one day it was announced that the United Nations had decided it would send troops to stop the war, which was, indeed, destroying a great deal of property, killing many citizens in both the warring countries, and possibly spreading to other nearby countries. The Winterses did not like the U.N. because they thought people in a community should help each other and themselves and not have outsiders come in to solve their problems for them. Mr. and Mrs. Winters felt sorry for those people, but believed it was their own responsibility to take care of themselves.

The next day their son called and said his army company was being sent as part of the United Nations' forces to stop the war in Europe. They realized their son might be killed.

What do you think the Winterses thought and did? What is your opinion of the Winterses?

14. Mary has been married to Joe for 20 years. They have four children whose ages are 8, 10, 13, and 17. Joe, who never completed high school, works in the warehouse of a big department store, lifting and carrying heavy boxes all day. He doesn't earn very much, but, because he is a very hard and excellent worker and has worked there for 19 years, he makes an adequate salary to support his family. The store also has good life insurance and retirement programs, so Joe is very happy and proud that he can provide for his family's security when he gets old or if he dies.

One day at work Joe makes a mistake and a big pile of boxes falls on him and he is killed. After several months, Mary calls the store to find out when she is going to get Joe's life insurance and retirement money. She has only $800 left in the bank and the house payment of $500 is due. Without Joe's salary the family will soon have no money even for food, and they will not be able to keep their home. The retirement and insurance money would be enough for them to live almost as well as when Joe was alive and working. But the store lawyer says there will be no retirement or life insurance because Joe's own mistake caused his death. Mary, who also never finished high school and who has never worked outside the home, asks a lawyer to help her. He looks at the retirement and insurance contracts and shows her that she will not be able to get Joe's retirement or insurance money because he caused his own death.

Mary makes an appointment with the president of the store and asks for help. You are the president of the store. What will you do and why?

15. A boatload of people from a war-torn country has landed illegally on a U.S. shore. These people are afraid for their lives and are asking for safety. Some U.S. citizens, however, say we have too many illegal aliens already and that our land has too much unemployment.

If you were on the government committee to make the decision as to whether these people could stay, what would your decision be? Why?

16. Once upon a time, a young woman gave her father a gift because she loved him very much. He told his daughter that he would keep his new gift forever. But the father was careless and forgot to put the gift where he could find it. After a few weeks he tried to find his new gift. However, the gift had disappeared, and he

was convinced that it had been stolen by a thief. He tried every way he could to find whoever might have stolen the gift. But he couldn't find it anywhere and no one had seen it. However, later someone remembered seeing a crow flying away with it. But how could the father find the gift if a crow had flown away with it? He felt very guilty and did not know what he would say if his daughter asked him about the gift. He was afraid his daughter would think he did not love her if he had not been careful with her gift. He was so afraid that she would ask him about the gift that he kept away from her. When the daughter saw her father staying away from her and not wanting to talk to her, she thought he did not love her anymore. They loved each other very much but never talked anymore and as a result both became very unhappy.

What is the lesson of this story?

SAMPLE PRETESTS
AND POSTTESTS

Here are typical pretests and posttests from a variety of students in classes using this **NHLP** curriculum. All errors have been retained.

These are excerpts from a pretest and posttest written by a man in his twenties who had been brain damaged during a childhood illness. The writing prompt was the same for both tests: "Write about one of your best classes."

PRETEST:

The best class I toke in high school was radio communication. it consisted of having good attendance and we had to take class notes but the teacher would only make us write notes that were on the board, we would watch movies every Friday....

POSTTEST:

The best class that I had taken in high school was radio communication. The way I found out about the class was from the student's school Directory that was given to me by my counselor. I was reading the Directory in my counselor's office when my Dad and I were there....

The following excerpts were written by a woman who had been out of school for eight years. The prompt for the pretest was to write about a favorite class. The prompt for the posttest was to respond to a moral dilemma concerning a student who had cheated on a writing assignment and was now facing expulsion for plagiarism (see prompt 11 in the preceding section). The students were asked what they thought the teacher should do and why.

PRETEST:

I liked the class because I new most of the people in it. the Teacher was very good he made it interesting and fun.... The atmospher was great it was fun and at times it was serious... You got to act out imporants parts in history.

POSTTEST:

Mike should have started his paper a lot earlier because he knew he would have a lot of things to do to get ready for graduate school. The teacher should try to understand all the pressure Mike was going through, rather than expel him from school. I think they should give him another chance provided that he knows about the plagiarism rule....

The following pretest and posttest were written by a second-language speaker who had returned to college after retirement. The prompt for the first test was to decide which of two students should receive the last remaining college scholarship, the athlete who is a poor student or the good student who is a poor athlete (see prompt 1 in the preceding section). The second prompt was a self-evaluation.

PRETEST:

I thing the scholarship should go to the person who hardly made it through high school. He is a good asthlic and, his family eager for him to go to college. At least he is good in some thing like football some people are good in studying some can do something else. So my opion he gets the scholarship, and the other smart poor boy he can make it in life.

POSTTEST:

I would like to write about what I learned in the Fall quarter. When I started the class I felt I wouldn't be able to handle it. Although it was hard for me, I learned a lot. Whatever the assignments were, I struggled through them. I have never written as many papers before this as I wrote in your class. I appreciate the hard work that you put in it. I know that my dendrites were asleep before I came to your class. Now, however, they are growing regularly. This class has been very helpful to me. Although my dendrites are growing, the rest of me is falling like the leaves on the trees. Now, at the end of the quarter I feel very tired and exhausted.

Here is the pretest and excerpts from the posttest of a young man who had been through a number of ESL courses. The prompt for the pretest was to write about his strengths and weaknesses as a writer and what he thought the purpose of writing is. The prompt for the postest was a moral dilemma adapted from Kohlberg (the Heinz dilemma): The wife of a poor man is dying and a druggist has a cure. But it is very expensive. The man cannot afford the medicine, so he steals it. He is caught and put on trial. The student's task is to say whether the man is guilty or not and, if guilty, what his punishment should be and why.

PRETEST:

As a writer I have a creativity mind, a lot of ideals and imaginations. My weakness as a writer that I want to improve is that I will be able to express that in writing so that other persons could understood me. I also need to study in grammar. Writing is express ourself to the people. It is a form of communication that we use it every day.

POSTTEST:

People say that the law is blind justice; it means justice doesn't distinguish the power and the wealth of each individual, but it judges him on the basis that if he has committed a crime, he is guilty for that crime whatever the circumstance. When someone has committed a crime, even a petty small crime, if he was judged by that blind justice, he will automatically be found guilty for that crime. The man, the husband of the dying woman, as we know, wants to save his wife's life; but he doesn't have any money to pay for the expensive drug which could eventually help his wife, and the druggist inhumanly refuses to help them even though the man promises to pay him back later. Therefore, in the desperate situation he will do any thing even foolishly to save his wife.

SAMPLES OF FEEDBACK ON ONE STUDENT'S HOMEWORK AND IN-CLASS ESSAYS

Eva Slaughter, the student, was a middle-aged woman returning to college. She completed homework for almost every class and wrote all the in-class essays. The following pages are selected from her body of work to demonstrate the kind of feedback suggested for this **NHLP** curriculum. Eva's progress through the quarter, facilitated not only by her own conscientious effort but also supported and guided by this type of feedback, shows the progress a student can make even in eleven weeks.

APRIL 2, 1991: EVA'S PRETEST ON THE FIRST DAY OF CLASS

Eva Slaughter   4-2-91

1. My Strength as a Student are Very minimun I need to Learn how to reLat and take more time to read.

2. My Problems as a Student are the Same as above

3. I would Like to Learn how to ConEecrate to Keep the miNe from Wondering while I am trying to read.
   about myseLF I am a Very hard worker, but I Love doing thing with my famiLy. My famiLy is Very nice, daughter marry soN going to College another soN Prinelpal List.

The prompt was to "write on your strengths as a student, your problems as a student, what you would like to learn in this class, and something about yourself." (This pretest has since been replaced with a complex moral dilemma, which stretches students to do complex thinking and precludes their writing about simple ideas in correct simple sentences.)

APRIL 2, 1991: EVA'S FIRST HOMEWORK ASSIGNMENT, DONE AFTER THE FIRST LESSON ON PREPOSITIONAL PHRASES

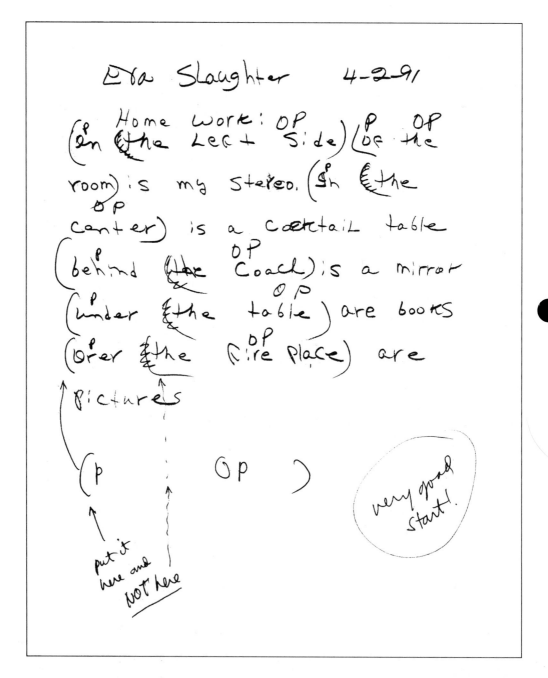

The prompt was to "describe where things are in your home. Analyze your prepositional phrases." Notice that Eva did not have a complete concept of a prepositional phrase; I crossed out her incorrectly placed parentheses and added parentheses at the start of the phrase. Also note the positive comment that this is a "very good start!" This was true (she analyzed every **P** and **OP** correctly). If she had not analyzed all of them correctly, I would have looked for one thing that I could have praised, because even one thing that is correct is an important guideline to help a student construct a new grammar neural network. Eva Slaughter was one of those students for whom the sentence is a mass of undifferentiated words; they need clear, specific guidelines so that they can begin to see the elements and structures of a sentence. At this point (before Chapter 7) no comment was made about her run-on sentences and lack of a period at the end. The teacher needs only to help shape the schema or concept under construction.

APRIL 4, 1991: EVA'S HOMEWORK ASSIGNMENT TWO DAYS LATER

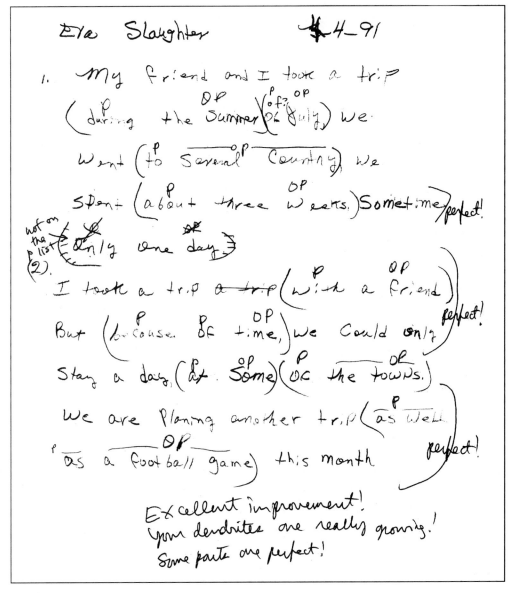

The prompt was to "write two to three sentences about anything of interest; it could be about an experience or one of the homework assignments given in the textbook. Analyze your prepositional phrases." She now had a firm concept of this structure and made only one error ("only" is not a preposition). Every "perfect!" was a guideline and support to help her continue to shape her understanding and tool use.

APRIL 5, 1991: EVA'S NEXT HOMEWORK ASSIGNMENT

The prompt was to "write three sentences using compounds. Analyze your prepositional phrases and compounds." Her serious error in the first sentence was not prematurely commented on at this point. Her grasp of compounds, however, was becoming quite refined and sophisticated.

APRIL 11, 1991: EVA'S HOMEWORK ASSIGNMENT A WEEK LATER

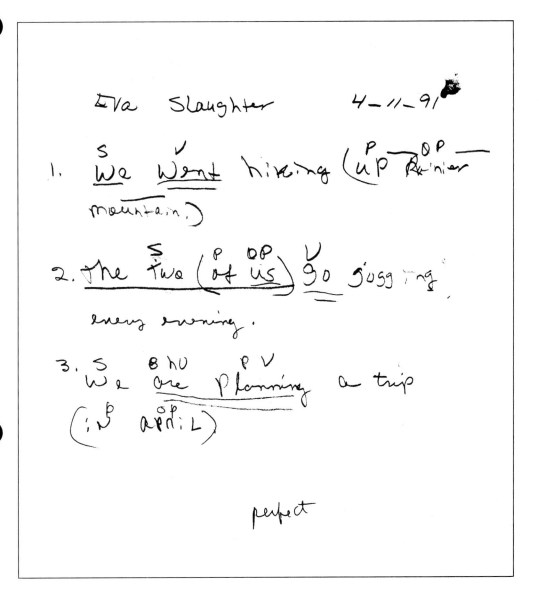

The prompt was the same as that for April 4, but now included analyzing subjects, verbs, helper verbs, and continuous participles, called "continuing verbs" (CV) in this curriculum. Eva now had clear concepts of all these elements. For example, she knew that "hiking" and "jogging" could not be the continuing verbs because "went" and "go" are not "be helper" verbs (BH). Later in the course she would be able to identify "hiking" and "jogging" as verbals.

APRIL 22, 1991: EVA'S HOMEWORK ASSIGNMENT ELEVEN DAYS LATER

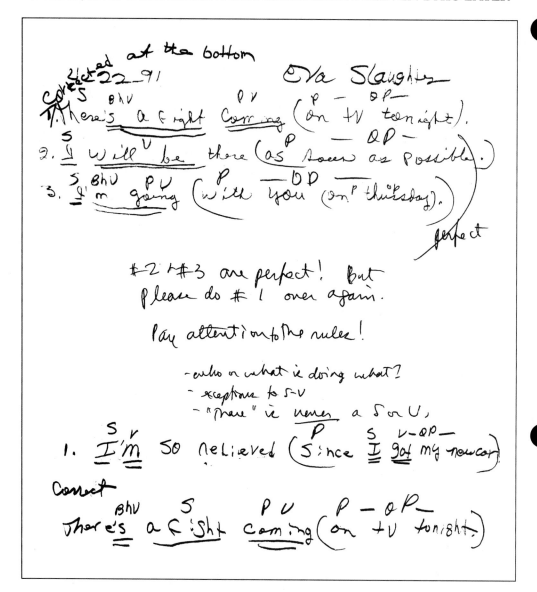

The prompt was the same as that for April 11. Notice that Eva corrected her first sentence at the bottom of the page, shaping and constructing a more refined neural network for subjects and verbs: **CV** = Continuing Verb (later she will learn to distinguish between the two different kinds of participles). Also notice that she had one prepositional phrase inside another one: (with you (on Thursday)). Finally, she is analyzing a dependent clause as a prepositional phrase, which is correct at this point because the concept of clauses has not yet been introduced.

MAY 10, 1991: EVA'S HOMEWORK SEVENTEEN DAYS LATER

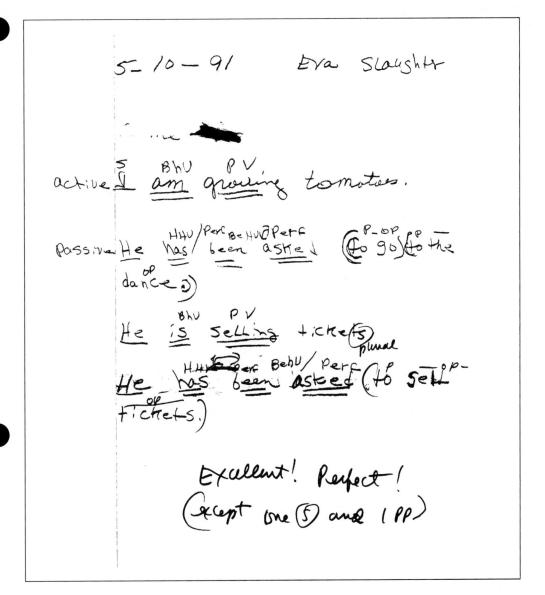

The prompt was to "write two active and passive verbs. Analyze all elements."
Notice that in her passive verbs Eva analyzed the three parts of the verb as

HV / PV BH / PV
has   been   asked

HH = Have Helper Verb
PV = Prestarted Verb (Perfect or Past Participle)
BH = Be Helper Verb

Eva showed that the middle verb was both the prestarted verb following the have helper verb as well as the be helper verb preceding the prestarted verb (for a passive verb). Although her verb network was shaping into one that is complex, Eva was, however, still not being totally careful, missing an "s" at the end of a plural noun and not analyzing her last phrase.

MAY 17, 1991: AN IN-CLASS ESSAY

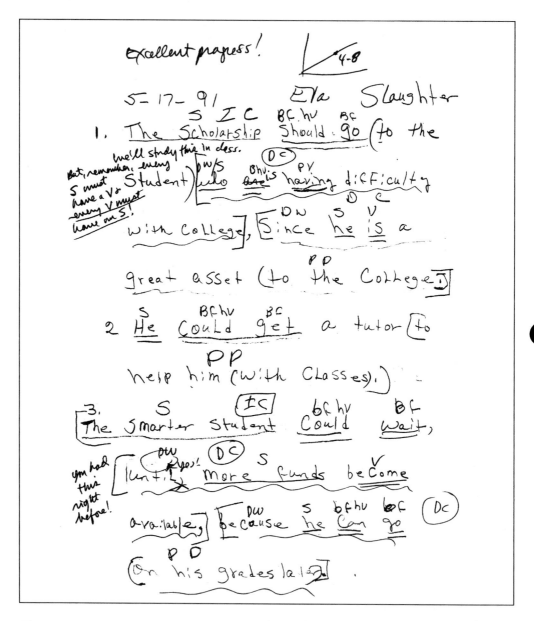

The prompt was a moral dilemma (all in-class essay prompts were given in this manual). The directions were to "write what you truly feel and think about the topic" and then analyze each sentence, correcting it if necessary. Notice that Eva was now identifying independent clauses (**IC**) and dependent clauses (**DC** with wavy underlining), showing her clear and more refined network for these structures. She is now also using **RH** and **RV** to analyze modals (root helper verbs) and root verbs. Also notice that the relative pronoun "who" was here analyzed as a dependent word (**DW**). As the note says, later she will be learning more about this **DW** (that it is a relative pronoun). The 4.8 is a grade on a scale of 0–6, using the **Natural Human Learning Process** scale.

JUNE 13, 1991: EVA'S FINAL EXAM:

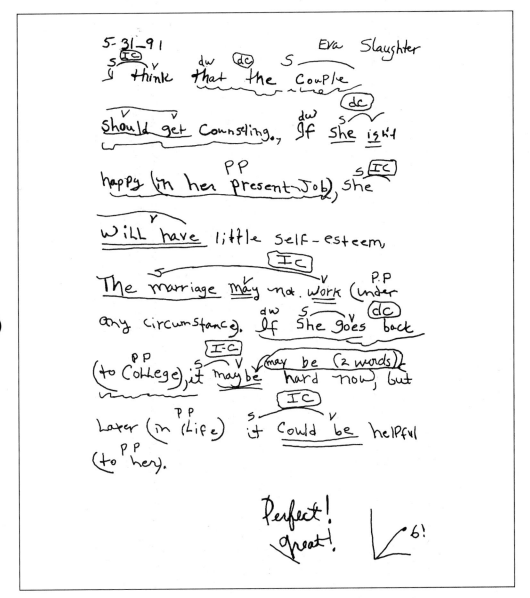

Contrasted with her pretest, this works shows Eva had become empowered to express her ideas in correct standard-code sentences and knew exactly what she was doing. Her spelling had also improved even though spelling was not studied in class.

SUPPLEMENTARY MATERIAL FOR CHAPTER 1:

"The Natural Process of Learning and Critical Thinking"

BY RITA SMILKSTEIN

In this paper I want to support my view that all our students (unless intellectually or emotionally impaired) are perfectly able to do abstract and critical thinking in all their classes. This view may seem to contradict the fact that some of our students do not catch on and do not think critically in our courses. And because some students do succeed, we reasonably assume the cause of lower achievement lies with the students who are doing the low achieving: Clearly, there must be something wrong with them or what they are doing.

Some educational theorists believe the lower-achieving students are people who have been slower to develop intellectually/cognitively than the higher-achieving students, and are simply less mature. Some theorists believe the lower-achieving students have low motivation, a poor attitude, less intelligence, and/or less aptitude for particular subjects or for college work in general than the higher-achieving students.

Any or all of these causes may explain why certain students can't make it to a high level of thinking in our courses. But what if all these students really are able to do critical thinking in our courses, and would be glad to do so, except that some obstacle outside themselves prevents them from doing so? This possibility cannot be overlooked.

After all, if they can speak—and probably learned to speak when they were around two years old—they have been operating at a high level of abstraction, skillfully using their critical and creative faculties, since the time they were six years old. To learn language, one of the most—if not the most—complex skills, children have to learn abstract language rules and structures. And this requires the innate ability to make and test hypotheses, synthesize, and solve problems, all of which are critical thinking activities and all of which children do naturally, without deliberate or conscious effort. This innate intellectual/cognitive capacity doesn't disappear as people get older; they simply may not be able to use it in the classroom. How to help students use their innate critical thinking capacity in our classrooms is one focus of this paper.

FIGURE 1 Steps of Learning, Recorded Verbatim		
Coordinated Studies Students	**Instructors in In-service Workshop**	**Basic Skills Students**
STEP 1		
Training, watching, ask questions, necessity, fear of it, experienced it, having fun with it, found it hard, modified expected results, forced into it, challenged, love of it, intrigued, humiliating, interest, fascinated	Trial & error, finding the problem, decide to do it, desire or need, motivation, observation, overcoming fear, lack of confidence, taught? *(The question mark signifies that one person contributed the item and others disagreed, but the originator wanted to keep it.)*	Have an interest, know you like it, God-given talent, creative?, practice, start basic
STEP 2		
Trial & error, development, followed instructions, practice, doing it, experiment, listening, read?, apprentice, loving it, failure, talking to others who have done it or doing it, discipline, exercises	Trust someone to help out, instruction, practice, experiment, trial & error, feedback from others, need or desire to improve, give self feedback	Practice, practice, practice; get comfortable; be pushed by others, challenge
STEP 3		
Becoming more comfortable, exercises, practice, sharpening skills, discovering own method, getting feedback, rewards	Experience, demonstration, evaluating, more trial & error, taking risks, beginning to go solo, imitate, creativity?	More practice, discipline, positive attitude, devotion, confidence, improving by adding new skills to it
STEP 4		
Recognition from others, can anticipate results, perfecting it, practice, doing it on own without support, expressing yourself through it, took lessons, becomes natural, feel a part of it, concentration	Refinement, confident, application, constant, go for it, deviate from what I've learned, creativity, spontaneity, improvisation, take risks, give self feedback	Keep it going, being inspired, being different from anyone else, branching out, creative
STEP 5		
Perfecting performance, total enjoyment, learning new methods, understanding why you're doing it, becomes second nature	Bridging, unique applications, using skill as building block, automaticity, internalization, further refinement, teach others, creativity, seeing cosmic connections, stop doing it and lose some skill	Good challenge, not giving it up, pushing yourself to keep going so no burnout, high pay/promotion, improvement, self-satisfaction, evaluate progress so far
STEP 6		
Maintenance/practice, learn to deal with problems, branch into secondary skills, knowing own limits, applying to other fields/broader application, enjoying it, increased creativity, feeling good, letting go of it, teaching others	— —	Mastering it, teaching it

My hypothesis is that cognitively unimpaired human beings have an innate learning system or process which makes it possible for us naturally to learn complex, abstract ideas and skills from an early age. When students don't achieve the same high level of learning in school as they did naturally when they were children or when they learn outside of school, it is because they are not learning naturally in school. In other words, 1) some school teaching doesn't give students the opportunity to do natural learning, and 2) some people can't learn unless they can learn naturally. To be clear, I am writing here about only the learning of new ideas and skills; and by "learning" I mean the ability to think about and use the new ideas and skills creatively and critically, as opposed to memorizing information by rote.

This hypothesis is the result of informal research I have been doing for the past eight years with about 1,000 people: low-achieving students, high-achieving students, and faculty in classrooms, faculty development workshops, and at local, state, and national conferences. I am going to describe the results of my research, but, to begin, here is a description of the research method I've used, and I welcome—and challenge—you to use this method with your own students so that you can see for yourselves that your students know very well how to learn a high level of expertise by the natural learning process. This procedure takes less than 50 minutes, so it can be done during one class session.

First, I ask participants (students in this case) to think of something they know how to do very well (e.g., swim, play guitar, carpentry, use a computer, write), making sure that everyone has a skill (if only driving a car) in mind before we continue. Then I ask them to write down what they went through from their first encounter with this skill until they got to be really good at it. They write for about three to five minutes—until the majority are finished. (I assure them this writing will be only notes for themselves and will not be read to the class nor collected by me.) I then have them, in small groups of three to four, read their processes to each other and compare to see whether there are any similarities in how they learned. This part of the procedure lasts for 10 to 15 minutes again, until a majority of the groups are finished.

Finally, with the group as a whole, I ask what happened at the beginning of their learning process. I write all their answers verbatim and without comment (except to clarify a point if necessary) on the chalkboard. When they have no more to say for this first part, I ask whether they are done with this part; when they say they are, I assure them they can add more later if anything else comes to mind as we go along. (Samples of the usual four to six stages are shown in Fig. 1) If someone objects to an item on the board—even if everyone but the originator of it objects—I leave it on the board but add a question mark.

Then I ask what they did next ("Was there another stage after that?") and, again, write verbatim what they report. This continues, stage by stage, until they say there are no more stages. Sometimes someone asks how many stages there are; my answer is that they are going to tell me.

FIGURE 2 Summary of Stages

STAGE 1 – *Motivation*: Responding to stimulus.

STAGE 2 – *Beginning Practice*: Doing it ("practice, practice, practice"), learning from one's own mistakes

STAGE 3 – *Advanced Practice*: Increase of skill and confidence through more practice, more trial & error, getting comfortable. *Foundation is built; only now can control, creativity, critical, and abstract thinking start for this new skill.*

STAGE 4 – *Skillfulness*: More practice, doing it one's own way, deviating from the norm, taking risks, creativity, branching out. Typically, taking lessons and reading appear here for the first time with the majority of the participants agreeing.

STAGE 5 – *Refinement*: Automization or becoming second nature, creativity, learning new methods, strong satisfaction.

STAGE 6 – *Mastery*: Increased creativity, broader application, teaching it, continuing improvement (or dropping the activity). In Figure 1 the instructor's group has no Step 6, but they have included Step-6-type of items in their Step 5 ("teach others," "seeing cosmic connections"). As noted above, whenever a group has fewer than six steps we see this type of telescoping of items.

When they are finished I ask, "Is this the way you learned your skill more or less, but more rather than less? Are there any changes or additions you want to make so that it represents the learning process you went through?" Then I read through the stages, which had been numbered as we went along, and invite them to fine-tune the stages so they fit their own experience as exactly as possible. Sometimes they will agree a particular item was present for all the stages (e.g., practice), so a horizontal arrow is drawn across all the stages. Also, I make the point that, as some participants have said, the stages actually flow into each other rather than one stage stopping and then the next stage starting.

This part of the informal research/orientation is not complete until everyone can sincerely agree this is more rather than less how he or she learned the skill. (Only one person of the approximately 1,000 who have participated in this research said he did not learn his skill at all by this process.)

My comment now is, "You learned all these different skills pretty much by this same process. Well, this is the learning process for members of our species. This is the natural human learning process. Since all of you are able to learn to this highest stage, all of you are very intelligent and your minds work perfectly. You can be assured that you are all capable of learning anything to the highest stage when you learn by this natural process." Needless to say, this is highly motivating for students, supporting or strengthening their self-esteem and confidence.

For every group of faculty and for every group of students, whether developmental or advanced, which has participated in this research, all have had four to six stages similar to the ones shown above. When there are four stages, it is easy to see the telescoping of six.

On the basis of this data—and similar data from hundreds of other classes and groups—it seems the natural human learning process has approximately six stages, which might be summarized (Fig. 2) though you can make your own summary of the data presented here or data from your own students.

Perhaps we can agree, if only for the sake of argument, that this is the natural human learning process. This means that critical or high-level thinking for a new topic, idea, or skill is possible only after Stage 3, after a sufficient amount of direct, personal, hands-on/written trial-and-error practice.

One of the most important insights we gain from this data is that essentially people learn by making and correcting (with helpful, supportive feedback from peers and teacher) their OWN mistakes. Both teachers and students must come to see and value the making of mistakes by learners. "That was a good mistake! It helps you learn because now you can see what you did wrong and have a better idea of the right way to see or do it." One of the greatest obstacles to learning is fear of making mistakes—which is the same as saying we fear the main thing needed for learning!

From the data it seems there are sequential stages of development in the learning of new skills and ideas, with higher stages following stage by stage from the preceding ones. To get to the higher ones, a person must first go through the lower ones.

These six sequential stages can be diagrammed (Fig. 3) (and I draw the following diagram on the chalkboard), starting from the bottom at stage one and working up to stage six. To clarify, this is the natural learning process for acquiring any and all new skills or ideas (not advanced study and not information that is to be memorized by rote).

Except for people with a special aptitude for a particular topic (the aptitude known by their learning something new more quickly and easily than others), learners can't start to creatively apply or think critically about or control or generalize a new skill or idea (at stages 4 to 6) until and unless there has first been a sufficient quantity of personal practice and trial and error learning (at stages 1 to 3). In other words, there seems to be a practice and time factor in learning.

Some clear implications are evident for instruction here. For example, when teachers, who are themselves at stage 6, lecture or assign readings at any level beyond the students' "ceiling level," the material will be over the students' heads (over their ceiling level).

The only students who can be expected to be high achievers in this situation are those few to whom the subject is not new and/or who are very highly motivated, extremely persevering, and have excellent study skills. All the other students can be expected to be lower achievers, through no fault of their own. One way to prevent this problem is to provide students with an opportunity to learn naturally so that they can all reach the stage where critical thinking naturally occurs in the learning of a new topic, idea, or skill.

That is, it helps students learn by their natural learning process when we give them opportunities (at stages 1–3) to practice doing or using the new idea or skill, making—and learning from—their own mistakes, rather than our telling and demonstrating while they merely listen, watch, and read. In other words, teachers cannot simply give their knowledge to students. Students must actively practice and learn from their own mistakes if they are to develop their own knowledge and skill to a high enough stage to do creative and critical thinking about that new idea or skill. At stages 4–6 students can first begin to benefit from teachers' lectures, because by then they will have a foundation of their own real understanding, which is a prerequisite for making authentic, critical sense and use of lectures and readings.

Research clearly shows—as does our experience—that students do not naturally transfer or generalize knowledge. Thus, if we want them to know something, it is that thing precisely that they must have the opportunity to practice through the six stages.

One way to begin a new topic (at stage 1) and at the same time ascertain the class ceiling level about the new topic, is to ask the students to write individually for a few moments on the question, "What do you know about [the topic]?" Then, as described earlier, we would have them, in groups of three to four, share and discuss what they know.

Finally, we would debrief them as a whole group, asking "What did you come up with?", writing their points verbatim and without comment on the board. When we finish we will have on the board an "x-ray picture" of the knowledge level of the class. A great instructional benefit of this procedure is that students are actively involved—in their writing, and in talking in small and large groups. Research shows that active student involvement is highly effective for learning. For this reason, I teach almost exclusively in this three-step sequence of individual task, small group sharing/discussion (where a great deal of powerful learning goes on), whole group debriefing. In almost every class I share the information in this

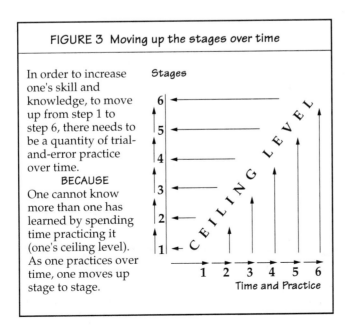

FIGURE 3 Moving up the stages over time

In order to increase one's skill and knowledge, to move up from step 1 to step 6, there needs to be a quantity of trial-and-error practice over time.

BECAUSE
One cannot know more than one has learned by spending time practicing it (one's ceiling level). As one practices over time, one moves up stage to stage.

Stages

Time and Practice

paper with my students. Whenever they begin a new unit and, of necessity, fall back to stage 1 for the new unit, I remind them of how the human mind naturally acquires new knowledge—stage by (active, trial-and-error) stage from 1 to 6 for every new idea or skill.

If this is the natural learning process, and if people can learn to high levels of critical and creative thinking by this process, then all intellectually and emotionally unimpaired students will be able to do critical thinking in every class in which they have the opportunity to be actively involved in the natural learning process.

BIBLIOGRAPHY OF BRAIN RESEARCH AND GRAMMAR RESEARCH

Bartholomae, D. (1980). The study of error. *College Composition and Communication, 31*, 253–269.

Bereiter, C. (1980). Development in writing. In L. W. Gregg & E. R. Steinberg (Eds.), *Cognitive processes in writing* (pp. 73–93). Hillsdale, NJ: Lawrence Erlbaum.

Bock, J. K. (1982). Toward a cognitive psychology of syntax: Information processing contributions to sentence formulation. *Psychological Review, 89,* 1–47.

Daiute, C. A. (1981). Psycholinguistic foundations of the writing process. *Research in the Teaching of English, 15,* 5–22.

Emig, J. (1981). Non-magical thinking: Presenting writing developmentally in schools. In C. H. Frederiksen & J. F. Dominic (Eds.), *Writing: The nature, development, and teaching of written communication.* Hillsdale, NJ: Erlbaum.

Fischbach, G. D. (1992). Mind and brain. *Scientific American, 267* (3), 48–57. A readable introduction to the physiology of the brain as it relates to learning. In fact, this whole issue of *Scientific American* would be a useful textbook on the brain.

Forrester, K. (1983). Why nothing works. *Teaching English in the Two-Year College, 5,* 16–22.

Garrett, M. F. (1981). Levels of processing in sentence production. In B. Butterworth (Ed.), *Language production* (pp. 177–220). New York: Academic Press.

Hartwell, P. (1985). Grammar, grammars, and the teaching of grammar. *College English, 5,* 105–127.

Heath, S. B. (1983). *Ways with words: Language, life, and work in communities and classrooms.* Cambridge, England: Cambridge University Press.

Hillocks, G. (1986). *Research on written composition.* Urbana, IL: National Conference on Research in English and ERIC. This is the most inclusive and detailed review of the literature on teaching writing, including teaching grammar.

Holbrook, H. T. (1983). ERIC/RCS Report: Whither (wither) grammar? *Language Arts, 5,* 159–263.

Hull, G., Rose, M., Fraser, K. C., & Castellano, M. (1991). Remediation as social construct: Perspectives from an analysis of classroom discourse. *College Composition and Communication, 42,* 299–329. Hull et al. demonstrate that teachers' implicit attitudes towards students have a powerful effect on the success of their students.

Jacobs, B., Schall, M., & Scheibel, A. B. (1993). A quantitative dendritic analysis of Wernicke's Area in humans. II. Gender, hemispheric, and environmental factors. *Journal of Comparative Neurology, 327,* 97–111. An important study about learning and the brain.

Kandel, E. R., & Hawkins, R. D. (1992). The biological basis of learning and individuality. *Scientific American, 267*(3), 78–86.

Kroll, B. M., & Vann, R. J. (1981). *Exploring speaking-writing relationships: connections and contrasts.* Urbana, IL: National Council of Teachers of English.

Milgram, N. W., MacLeod, C. M., & Petit, T. L. (1987) *Neuroplasticity, learning and memory.* New York: Alan R. Liss.

Noguchi, R. R. (1991). *Grammar and the teaching of writing.* Urbana, IL: National Council of Teachers of English.

Petit, T. L. & Markus, E. J. (1987) The cellular basis of learning and memory: The anatomical sequel to neuronal use. In N. W. Milgram, C. M. MacLeod, & T. L. Petit (Eds.), *Neuroplasticity, learning, and memory.* New York: Alan R. Liss, Inc. An important work on learning and the brain.

Piaget, J. (1970). *Genetic epistemology.* New York: W. W Norton.

Piaget, J. (1970). *Structuralism.* New York: Harper & Row.

Restak, R. M. (1979). *The brain: The last frontier.* New York: Warner. A readable general introduction to the brain.

Rose, M. (1988). Narrowing the mind and page: Remedial writers and cognitive reductionism. *College Composition and Communication, 39,* 267–302. Rose argues against the view, held by many, that basic/developmental writers are intellectually inferior or cognitively undeveloped. He argues that these students are capable thinkers but have not yet had the opportunity to learn the skills needed for proficiency in writing.

Shaunessy, M. P. (1977). *Errors and expectations: A guide for the teacher of basic writing.* New York: Oxford University Press. The seminal book that argued that developmental students are capable and intelligent but are just beginners in learning how to write correctly.

Taylor, S. J. (1986). Grammar curriculum—Back to square one. *English Journal, 75,* 94–98.

BRAIN-BASED EVALUATION INSTRUMENT

The Evaluation forms on the next pages are provided as additional, optional self-evaluation instruments. These instruments can be duplicated and given to the students to fill out. The first instrument is to be used *after* a chapter has been completed. The second is to be used *before* beginning the next chapter.

Using these forms strengthens students' metacognitive awareness in general and, specifically, their understanding that they must actually grow structures in their brain in order to learn—and that growing these structures (learning) is under their own control.

See sample student evaluations in this manual.

Name_____   Date_____

Self-Evaluation after Completing a Chapter

Here are some cell bodies. Draw on them what you think are the length and amount of the dendrites you have for the tools you studied in the last chapter. Refer to Figure 5 to get an idea of what your dendrites might look like at this point. Then, in the space below tell why you have this length and amount of dendrites.

Name_____   Date_____

Self-Evaluation before the Next Chapter

Here are some cell bodies. Draw on them what you think are the length and amount of the dendrites you have for the tools you will be learning in the next chapter. To find out what you will be learning in the next chapter, look at the list of "key terms" on the first page of that chapter. Then, in the space below, tell why you have this length and amount of dendrites.

Transparency Masters

for

Tools

Prepositions (P) are on the "Preposition List." They are never on the "Never a Preposition List."

Prepositions (P) can *never* have "a," "an," or "the" in front of them.

TOOL 3

Ask "what?" or "whom?" after a preposition (P). If there is an answer, the answer is the object of the preposition (OP). If there is no answer (no OP), then there is no preposition (no P). Use your own logic to decide what the answer is.

What a word is in a sentence depends on how it is used in that sentence.

TOOL 5

The object of the preposition (OP) stops at the end of the *whole* answer to "what?" or "whom?" asked after the preposition (P). Use your logic to know where the object of the preposition (OP) ends.

There can be two prepositions (P) in a row. Ask "what?" or "whom?" after both together.

A prepositional phrase (PP) is two or more words that logically go together. It starts with a P and ends with an OP. Use your logic to know which words go together.

If there are two or more PP's in a row, you can analyze them as separate PP's, or you can analyze them as going together. Do it the way that is most logical for you.

Harcourt Brace & Company

TOOL 9

If you know what infinitives (INF) are, you may analyze them as infinitives (INF) or as prepositional phrases (PP). We will study infinitives (INF) in Chapter 4.

Harcourt Brace & Company

A connector (C) joins two or more of the *same kind of things* that come before and after the connector (C): "and" and "or" are always connectors (C); "but" and ";" are sometimes connectors (C).

Number the things being connected.

Two same items connected by a connector (C) are called a "compound," such as compound preposition (cP), compound object of the preposition (cOP), and compound prepositional phrase (cPP).

Two or more same items in a compound are always in a list. Every item in a compound list must make sense when it is read alone with the rest of the sentence. Make sure you know where the compound list starts.

TOOL 13

To find the subject (S) and the verb (V), ask, "Who or what is, was, or will be doing something?" The whole answer to "who?" or "what?" is the subject (S). Put S over the subject (S) and underline it once.

What the subject (S) is doing is the verb (V). Analyze by putting V over the verb and underlining it twice.

TOOL 15

A subject (S) and its verb (V) must *both* be inside or *both* outside the same PP. No word inside a PP can be used with a word outside its PP. Words inside a PP can work only with words inside the *same* PP:

$$(S)V \quad - \quad No$$
$$S(V) \quad - \quad No$$
$$(SV) \quad - \quad Yes$$

TOOL 16

Verbs (V) that end in "ing" must have a "be" verb with them. They are called "continuing verbs" (CV). "Continuing" means the activity of the verb (V) is continuing over a period of time. The "be" helper verb (BH) and its continuing verb (CV) go together to make the whole verb: BH + CV = V.

Note: There are nine "be" verbs.

"Be" Helper Verbs

am, are, is, was, were, will be, been, being ("being" helps a different verb (V); more on this later)

Every "be" verb is always a verb (V). A "be" verb is either a verb (V) by itself or a "be" helper verb (BHI). There are two exceptions: "been" and "being." These are *never* verbs (V) by themselves; they are only helper verbs (HV). "Be" is a verb (V) by itself only in a command or a request: Be here at 4:00.

Both the subject (S) and the verb (V) must be singular (s), or both must be plural (p). This is called "number agreement." This is one of the most important tools.

TOOL 19

There can be only one subject (S) for each verb (V) and only one verb (V) for each subject (S)—unless there is a compound subject (CS) or a compound verb.

Note: No word inside a PP can be used with a word outside its PP. Words inside a PP can work only with other words inside the *same* PP.

Put a connector (C) between subject-verb pairs just as between any other compounds. Put a comma before the connector.

Harcourt Brace & Company

Without a "be" verb on the left helping it, the "ing" verb-like word is not a verb (V) in that sentence. It is a verbal (VBL) instead. A verbal (VBL) can be a subject (S) or an object of the preposition (OP).

A verb (V) can never be a description of the subject (S). A verb (V) tells what the subject (S) is doing or else it is a "be" verb.

Subject (S) and verb (V) are normally in the order of subject (S) first and then the verb (S-V or S-HV-V).

Words can come between the subject (S) and the verb (V).

TOOL 24

There are some exceptions to Tool 23.

a. Usually when "there" or "here" comes first, the order is V-S or HV-S-V. "There" and "here" are never subjects (S) or verbs (V).

b. In a question the order can be S-V, V-S, or HV-S-V.

Harcourt Brace & Company

There is a family of helpers called "root helper verbs" (RH):

can, could, did, do, does, may, might, must, shall, should, will, would.

Root helper verbs (RH) go with root verbs (RV).

When a root verb (RV) has no root helper verb (RH) and no subject (S) to the left of it, it might be a root verbal (RVbl).

When we give a command or a request, the subject (S) is an understood or invisible "you" because "you" is who will do the verb (V).

When we give a command or a request and address the person by name, that name is called the "addressing word" (AW). Separate the addressing word (AW) from the rest of the sentence with commas.

TOOL 30

There are two kinds of verbs (V): regular and irregular. All regular verbs have the same past tense verb and prestarted verb (PV). They both always end in "ed." Irregular verbs usually have a different past tense verb and prestarted verb (PV), and they do not end in "ed."

Harcourt Brace & Company

There are four "have" helper verbs (HHH): have, has, had, will have.

They go with prestarted verbs (PV) to make a whole verb (V).

Harcourt Brace & Company

If there is no "have" helper verb (HH) and no subject (S), then the word that looks like a prestarted verb (PV) is really a prestarted verbal (PVbl).

A verb (V) is called "active" when the subject (S) does the verb (V).

TOOL 34

A verb (V) is called "passive" when someone or something else does the verb (V) to the subject (S). The passive verb is always a "be" helper verb + prestarted verb (BH + PV). The someone or something that does the verb (V) to the subject (S) is always in a prepositional phrase (PP) starting with "by." This PP can be written in the sentence or can be understood and invisible.

When three or four verbs (V) are used in a row, a verb (V) that is between two other verbs (V) is both a helper verb (HV) and a main verb (V)

RH   RV/HH   PV

I could have done it.

Some subjects (S) and verbs (V) can be combined into one word by leaving out one or more letters. An apostrophe indicates that a letter or letters are left out.

TOOL 37

After the subject (S) and its verb (V), ask, "Whom or what?" The answer is the subject-verb completer (SVC). Use your sense of logic to decide what the *whole* subject-verb completer (SVC) is. A subject-verb completer (SVC) is. A subject-verb completer (SVC) can be short or long.

The first word of a subject-verb completer (SVC) is sometimes a continuing verbal (CVbl) or a perfect verbal. Use the continuing verbal (CVbl) for an *action*. Use the perfect verbal for a *description*.

TOOL 39

The first words of a subject-verb completer (SVC) are never a subject (S) and verb (V). The verb-like word is really only a verbal (Vbl). There is an exception—when the first word after the verb (V) is one of the following words, it is a subject (S), and it does have a verb (V):

who, whoever, what, whatever, which, whichever, and sometimes that

TOOL 40

A pronoun is a word that refers to a previous word (noun) that is a subject (S), an object of the preposition (OP), or a subject-verb completer (SVC). A pronoun might also refer to a whole statement (They discussed science, and it was a stimulating conversation). The previous word or statement the pronoun refers to is called its "referent." A pronoun's referent needs to be close behind it so it is clear what the referent is.

TOOL 41

A pronoun has a different form according to whether it is a subject (S) or not a subject (S). The different forms are called "cases."

a. When the pronoun is a subject (S) = subjective case (SC) = I, we, you, he, she, it, they, who, whoever.

b. When the pronoun is not a subject (S) = objective case (OC) = me, us, you, him, her, it, them, whom, whomever.

c. Pronouns that do not change their form = either a subject (S) or not a subject = you, it, this, that, these, those, what, whatever, which, whichever.

When the verb (V) is one of the "be" verbs, a pronoun subject-verb completer (SVC) has the same case as the subject (S) (subjective case [SC]).

Every pronoun and its referent must both be singular (s), or they must both be plural (p). This is called "pronoun number agreement."

Clauses and phrases are two main parts or structures of a sentence. A clause is two or more words that go together and always has one and only one subject-verb pair in it. A phrase is two or more words that go together and never has a subject-verb pair in it. A phrase can be inside a clause.

TOOL 45

There are only two kinds of clauses: independent clauses (IC) and dependent clauses (DC). The only difference between independent (IC) and dependent clauses (DC) is that dependent clauses (DC) always start with a dependent word (DW) and independent clauses (IC) never start with one. The subject-verb in an independent clause (IC) is called the "independent subject-verb" (ISV); it is the most important element in a sentence.

Identify a dependent word (DW) by these tests:

1. it's on the list

2. when you ask "what?" after it, there is an answer

3. there is a subject-verb pair after it that answers the question "what?"

Harcourt Brace & Company

TOOL 46 (continued)

Many of these words are also on the list of prepositions (P). The word is a dependent word (DW) or a preposition (P) depending on whether there is a subject-verb after it in that particular sentence.

a. "If" can be used for something that definitely isn't true (use "if–were–would" together) and also for something whose truth we aren't certain about.

A dependent clause (DC) at the start of a sentence has a comma after it. A dependent clause (DC) in the middle of a sentence starts and ends with commas. There is one exception: dependent clauses (DC) that begin with "how," "that," "what," and "why" never have commas.

TOOL 48

Most dependent clauses (DC) give extra information that is movable and/or removable. They can be moved to other places, or they can be removed from the sentence altogether and the sentence will still be grammatically correct. However, whatever starts a sentence will seem the most important idea in the sentence to the readers.

There are *never* two dependent words (DW) in a row. When there are two dependent words (DW) in a row, each one must have its own subject-verb pair, and one dependent clause (DC) will be inside another one.

TOOL 50

The word "that" is a tricky word. It can be used differently in different sentences. It can be: a subject (S), a dependent word (DW), a subject (S) *and* a dependent word (DW) at the same time, a subject-verb completer (SVC), an object of the preposition (OP), or a word that goes with another word (adjective [ADJ]).

There is one invisible dependent word (DW): "that." The invisible "that" can never start a sentence.

Harcourt Brace & Company

TOOL 52

After a mental action verb, usually "that" is the dependent word (DW) that follows it. Often "that" is invisible.

Some mental action verbs are: know, think, dream, say, believe, understand, feel.

Harcourt Brace & Company

If you can replace the word "that" with the word "this," "that" is not a dependent word (DW).

Harcourt Brace & Company

TOOL 54

When a sentence looks like it has more than one independent clause (IC), try to add "that" before each subject-verb pair. If it makes sense, then "that" is an invisible dependent word (DW) and the clause is a dependent clause (DC).

TOOL 55

There are only four kinds of sentences.

a. If a sentence has only one independent clause (IC), it is called a "simple sentence." A simple sentence may have one or more prepositional phrases (PP) in it.

b. If a sentence has one independent clause (IC) and also one or more dependent clauses (DC), it is called a "complex sentence."

Harcourt Brace and Company

TOOL 55 (continued)

c. If a sentence has two independent clauses (IC) and they are correctly separated (see Tool 56), it is called a "compound sentence." It does not matter how many dependent clauses (DC) there are (there can be none or several).

d. Sometimes one or both of the sentences in the compound sentence are complex sentences. Then the compound sentence is called a "compound-complex sentence."

TOOL 56

For sentences to be grammatically correct, 1) every sentence must have at least one independent clause (IC) and 2) all independent clauses (IC) must be separated from each other by one of the eleven independent clause separators (ICS).

The following four marks of punctuation and seven words are the only ways to separate independent clauses (IC):

End punctuation: .   !   ?   ;

Word with comma: , and   , but   , or

,nor   ,yet   ,for   ,so

Harcourt Brace and Company

TOOL 57

Dependent clauses (DC) do not matter when you are making sure a sentence is grammatically correct. Only the independent clauses (IC) matter. You may have as many dependent clauses (DC) as you want. But you must use this tool to be sure you have the correct number of independent clauses (IC). This is one of the most important tools.

a. Every sentence must have at least one independent clause (IC).

b. Every independent clause (IC) must be correctly separated from every other independent clause (IC).

c. Count the number of subject-verb pairs. That's how many clauses there are. There can be only one independent clause (IC) on each side of an independent clause separator (ICS).

TOOL 58

Whenever a sentence does not contain an independent clause (IC), it is a sentence crime called a "fragment." Correct a fragment by adding an independent subject-verb pair (ISV) to it or by joining it to the independent clause (IC) next to it.

Harcourt Brace and Company

TOOL 59

Whenever two independent clauses (IC) are not separated by anything, it is a sentence crime called a "run-on." Correct a run-on by putting an independent clause separator (ICS) between the independent clauses (IC) (use Tool 56) or by adding a dependent word (DW) or by seeing whether there is an invisible "that" as an invisible dependent word (DW).

Harcourt Brace and Company

TOOL 60

Whenever two independent clauses (IC) are separated by only a comma, it is a sentence crime called a "comma splice."

Correct a comma splice by putting an independent clause separator (ICS) between the independent clauses (IC) (use Tool 56) or by adding a dependent word (DW).

Harcourt Brace and Company

A dependent clause (DC) can be a subject (S), a part of an object of the preposition (OP), or a subject-verb completer (SVC). When a dependent clause (DC) is used this way, it does not have commas around it.

TOOL 62

When a subject-verb pair is placed in the middle or at the end of a sentence just to tell what someone is thinking, saying, or feeling about what the sentence says, they are just "words alone" (WA) and not a regular subject-verb pair. They are separated from the rest of the sentence by commas. "Words alone" (WA) will always become the subject (S) and the verb (V) if they are moved to the start of the sentence. "That" does not make sense before "words alone" (WA).

--WA--
<u>This is</u>, I think, the best class.

Harcourt Brace and Company

Some dependent words (DW) are special. They are pronouns that relate back to a "referent" (antecedent) that comes just before them. They are called "relative words" (RW), and their dependent clauses (DC) are called "relative clauses" (RC).

Some relative words (RW) can be both
a relative word (RW) and also the
subject (S) of its relative clause (RC).

Harcourt Brace and Company

Sometimes the relative word (RW) "that" will be invisible. Both visible "that" and the invisible "that" are correct. (Use either one as you prefer.) But the invisible relative word (RW) "that" can *never* be the subject (S) of its clause.

Do not analyze a relative word (RW) as such in a question that starts with that relative word (RW). The question is not a relative clause (RC).

Four relative words (RW) have "case": who, whoever, whom, whomever.

If they are the subject (S), they are in the subjective case (SC) (who, whoever). If not, they are objective case (OC) (whom, whomever).

TOOL 68

A relative word (RW) that is the subject (S) of its clause must have the same number as its referent. Be sure to identify the correct referent.

Harcourt Brace and Company

A relative dependent clause (DC) describes or identifies its referent.

TOOL 70

A relative clause (RC) must come immediately after its referent. When the clause does not come immediately after its referent, it is called a "misplaced modifier." This is a very serious mistake.

A short prepositional phrase (PP) can come between a relative clause (RC) and its referent, but the meaning must be completely clear.

Harcourt Brace and Company

TOOL 71

A dependent clause (DC) uses commas according to where the dependent clause (DC) is. But a relative clause (RC) uses commas only if the clause is nonessential for knowing exactly which person or thing the referent is. If the relative clause (RC) is essential to know exactly which person or thing the referent is, it does *not* use commas.

a. If the meaning of the sentence would still be clear if the relative clause (RC) were erased, then it is just interesting, extra information and has commas. But if the information in the relative clause (RC) is essential for the meaning of the sentence, then it does *not* have commas.

Punctuate compound lists of three or more subjects (S), verbs (V), objects of prepositions (OP), and subject-verb completers (SVC) by this pattern:

A, B, and C

A, B, C, and D

TOOL 73

When there are only two items in a list, never use both a comma and a connector (C).

the long, and interesting book   No

the long, interesting book   Yes

To see whether a comma should be used in a list, try using the word "and" instead. If the "and" makes logical sense, then you can use a comma.

If one of the items in a list has its own commas, separate the items with semicolons instead of commas or else the list will be too confusing.

Adjectives (Adj) describe or tell about subjects (S), objects of prepositions (OP), and subject-verb completers (SVC).

Adjectives (Adj) tell "what kind," "how many," and "how it compares."

Adjectives (Adj) can go before the word they give information about.

There is no comma between the adjective (Adj) and the word it is giving information about.

Adjectives (Adj) can go after the word they give information about. Then they are called "appositives" (App). Commas must separate appositives (App) from the rest of the sentence.

TOOL 81

Adverbs (Adv) give extra information about verbs (V), verbals (Vbl), adjectives (Adj), and other adverbs (Adv). The following words are always adverbs (Adv):

very, really, well.

Adverbs (Adv) tell how, when, where, and how much.

Adverbs (Adv) can go before or after the word they give information about.

TOOL 84

When writers want to tell exactly what someone said, they put quotation marks around the exact words that were said. Commas and periods are always to the left of the quotation marks.

She said, "I will be going with you."

If a writer doesn't use the exact words, quotation marks are not used. This is called a "paraphrase."

She said she will be coming along with us.

Harcourt Brace and Company

TOOL 85

There are three steps to spelling a possessive word correctly:

1. Write the correct singular (s) or plural (p) spelling of the possessor word:

The Possessor Word	What the Possessor Possesses
a book (singular)	pages
several books (plural)	covers

Harcourt Brace and Company

2. Add "'s" (apostrophe + "s") to the end of the possessor word:

a book's   pages

several books's   covers

3. If there is more than one "s," erase the last "s." (There are two different correct styles. This is one of them.)

a book's   pages

several books'   covers

Some pronouns are used for possession. Some possessive pronouns can never be used alone, and some can be used alone:

Never Used Alone			Can Be Used Alone		
my	her		mine	his	theirs
our	their		ours	hers	whose
your			yours	its	

Harcourt Brace and Company

Possessive pronouns *never* use an apostrophe (your, his, hers, its, theirs):

Its tail was wagging. Yours are ready.

TOOL 88

Apostrophes are used for only three purposes:

a. in contractions: he is ⟶ he's

b. for possession (except pronoun possessives; see Tools 86-87): Norma's room, parties' entertainment

c. for plurals of nonwords: There are two "3's" in her phone number.

TOOL 89

Words end in "s" for only five reasons:

a. The word is normally spelled with an "s" at the end: fuss, confess.

b. Almost every present tense verb with a singular (s) subject (S) that is not "I" or "you" and is singular (s) ends in "s"; for example, I work, you work, she works. (Root helper verbs (RH) do not end in "s" except "does.") (Also see Tool 96.)

c. When the verb (V) is the "be" verb, it ends in "s" in the past tense when the subject (S) is any singular (s) subject (S) except "you": I was, you were, he was.

TOOL 89 (continued)

d. Many singular (s) nouns become plural (p) by adding an "s," "es," or "ies"; for example:

book ——→ books

mess ——→ messes

lady ——→ ladies.

Students will need to use a dictionary to see which words need "s," "es," or "ies" (or a different spelling of the words) to become plural (p); for example:

sheep ——→ sheep

mouse ——→ mice

ox ——→ oxen.

e. Possessive words (except pronouns) usually end in "s" (see Tools 85 and 87).

TOOL 90

There are four more exceptions to the normal word order of S-V.

a. The normal word order of subject-verb (S-V) is reversed often after "not . . . , nor" and "not . . . , and neither." Be sure to include the comma.

I did not go, nor did Ted.

I did not go, and neither did Ted.

b. The normal word order of subject-verb (S-V) is usually reversed after "not only." A comma (or comma + "but") must come before a second subject-verb (S-V). You may choose to add "also" to the second part.

Not only <u>did</u> I <u>go</u>, but <u>Ted</u> also <u>went</u>.

Harcourt Brace and Company

TOOL 90 (continued)

c. After ", and so" the word order is verb-subject (V-S), but only when the parts before and after ", and so" are saying that the two subjects (S) did the same thing. The comma is part of this tool.

I <u>went</u>, and so <u>did</u> Ted.

d. Sometimes when a prepositional phrase (PP) is in front, the word order can be V-S or HV-S-V.

(Under the pile of papers) <u>was</u> her lost book.

TOOL 91

Self-referring case (SRC) pronouns are used to emphasize whom the writer is referring to or to say that a noun is doing something for himself, herself, itself, themselves, etc.

SRC

They <u>did</u> it themselves.

Some pronouns are always singular (s). Other pronouns are always plural (p). And other pronouns can be singular (s) or plural (p) depending on the sentence.

Singular	Plural	Singular or Plural
I he she	we they	you
me him her	us them	who

A pronoun must always have the same number as its referent.

They are the students [who work hard].

--PLURAL--

[------RC------]

RW/S
--PLURAL--

She is the student [who works hard].

Singular

[------RC------]

RW/S
--SINGULAR--

TOOL 94

Every subject (S) has person. This means the subject (S) is either first person (1) (I, we), second person (2) (you), or third person (3) (he, she, it, they; third person [3] is also everyone and everything that is not "I," "we," "you").

A compound subject (CS) including "I" is first person plural (1p).

Harcourt Brace and Company

The verb (V) must have the same person as its subject (S). This is called "agreement of person."

Almost every verb (V) in the third singular present has "s," "es," or "ies" at the end. Root helper verbs (RH), however, do not end in "s" except for "does."

A verb's (V) tense tells when the verb (V) happens; use present tense for verbs (V) that happen usually or always, past tense for verbs (V) that happened before, and future tense for verbs (V) that will happen later.

Verbs (V) that happen at the *same time* must have the *same tense*. If they happen at *different times*, they must have *different tenses*. This is called "tense agreement."

The "be" verb is the most irregular verb (V) in English (see Tools 16 and 17). There are three different forms for the present tense (am, is, are). Also, "be" is the only verb (V) that has two forms for the singular (s) past (was, were).

TOOL 100

In a compound subject (S) with "or" as the connector (C), the number of the verb (V) is singular (s) or plural (p) based on the number of the last subject (S) before the verb (V).

TOOL 101

To name the tense of a verb (V) with more than one part, name the tense of the helper verb (HV) (past, present, or future) and then name the main verb (V) (continuing [CV] or prestarted [PV]). The root verb (RV) does not have a tense name, and root helper verbs (RH) have no tense except for the following: did, do, does, will, shall (see Tool 101g).

PRESENT CONTINUING
We <u>are going</u>.

Harcourt Brace and Company

TOOL 101 (continued)

a. When the verb (V) tells what is continuing to happen right now, the "be" helper verb (BH) is present tense and the main verb (V) is a continuing verb (CV).

b. When the verb (V) tells what was continuing to happen in the past, the "be" helper verb (BH) is past tense and the main verb (V) is a continuing verb (CV).

Harcourt Brace and Company

TOOL 101 (continued)

c. When the verb (V) tells what will be continuing to happen in the future, the "be" helper verb (BH) is future tense and the main verb (V) is a continuing verb (CV).

d. When the verb (V) tells what started in the past and still happens, the "have" helper verb (HH) is present tense and the main verb (V) is a prestarted verb (PV).

e. When the verb (V) emphasizes that
something happened before something else
happened later in the past, the "have"
helper verb (HH) is past tense (had) and the
main verb (V) is a prestarted verb (PV).
This is the only use for "had" as a helper
verb (HH).

TOOL 101 (continued)

f. When the verb (V) tells what will happen before something else happens later in the future, the "have" helper verb (HH) is future tense and the main verb (V) is a prestarted verb (PV).

Note: If you use a second verb (V) to say what will happen later in the future, use a present tense verb (V) in a dependent clause (DC):

He will have practiced an hour [before class begins].

TOOL 101 (continued)

g. Root helpers (RH) have no tense except for the following:

did, do, does, shall, will.

h. English verbs have twelve common tenses.

In English there are three articles: a, an, the.

a. Articles go before almost every specific subject (S), subject-verb completer (SVC), and object of the preposition (OP). If there is no article, there usually must be a word telling how many: one, ten, some, many, any, etc.

b. General things usually do not have an article. (Justice is important.)

Harcourt Brace and Company

c. Articles usually go before a person's title (the professor). But they usually do not go before the title with the name (Professor Li, not the Professor Li).

d. Articles usually do not go before the proper name of a person, city, or state (Gerry, Seattle, Iowa). But articles usually do go before the proper name of a building or a structure (the Eiffel Tower).

e. When a nation's name is actually just a description (the United Kingdom: what kind of Kingdom? a united one) instead of a particular name (Britain), it must have an article.

TOOL 103

a. "The" can be used for singular (s) or plural (p). Use "the" to mean "this or that specific one" (singular) or "these or those specific ones" (plural). This is called a "definite article" (definite = specific).

b. use "a" and "an" to mean "any one" or "some sort of." This is called an "indefinite article" (indefinite = not so specific).

a. Use "a" when the next word starts with a consonant: *b, c, d, f, g, j, k, l, m, n, p, q, r, s, t, v, w, x, y, z*, and sometimes *h* (only when it has the "h" sound: a hat, an honor. This makes pronunciation easier).

b. Use "an" when the next word starts with a vowel: *a, e, i, o*, and sometimes *u* (only when it has an "uh" sound: an umbrella, a unit).

When a verb-like word comes after "to," normally use a root verbal (RVbl). This is an infinitive (Inf).

RVbl

They plan (to study).

When a verb-like word comes after
any preposition (P), except the
preposition (P) "to," normally use the
continuing verbal (CVbl).

CVbl

They thought (about studying).

TOOL 107

Two verbs (V) are used in a row only when the first one is a helper verb (HV). If you write two verb-like words in a row and the first is not a helper verb (HV), put "to" in front of the second verb-like word and make it a root verbal (RVbl). Add "to" even when other words are between the verb (V) and/or verbal (Vbl).

RH   RV
He might help them.
RVbl/Inf

Incorrect: He goes always help them.

Correct: He goes always (to help them.)

There are exceptions to Tool 107. (Study them in the "Toolbook.")

Some words are followed by "to" with a continuing verbal (CVbl). (See examples in the "Toolbook.")